real weddings

real weddings

a celebration of personal style

text by
SALLY KILBRIDGE

photographs by
MALLORY SAMSON

CLARKSON POTTER/PUBLISHERS

NEW YORK

REAL WEDDINGS

Copyright © 1999 by Sally Kilbridge and Mallory Samson

Photo on page 141 by Michelle Pattee.

Published by Clarkson N. Potter, Inc.
201 East 50th Street
New York, New York 10022
Member of the Crown Publishing Group

Random House, Inc.
NEW YORK, TORONTO, LONDON, SYDNEY, AUCKLAND
www.randomhouse.com

CLARKSON N. POTTER, POTTER, and colophon
are trademarks of Clarkson N. Potter, Inc.

Printed in China

Design by Spot Design

Library of Congress Cataloging-in-Publication Data
Real weddings : a celebration of personal style / text by Sally Kilbridge;
photographs by Mallory Samson.—1st ed.
Includes index.
1. Weddings—United States—Case studies. 2. Weddings—United States—Pictorial works.
3. Weddings—United States—Planning. I. Title
HQ745.K45   1999
395.2'2—dc21   98–19138

ISBN 609-60234-9

10 9 8 7 6 5 4 3 2 1

FIRST EDITION

To my very patient family, friends, and colleagues.
— SALLY KILBRIDGE

To the memory of Bea Feitler and Betty Boote, both of
whom had faith in me from the beginning of my career, and
to David Dowd, who challenged me to follow my heart.
And with gratitude to my parents for their love and support.
— MALLORY SAMSON

contents

 home-inspired weddings

 heritage-inspired weddings

acknowledgments

In addition to the couples and wedding professionals whose generosity with their time allowed this book to come to life, we would like to thank Lauren Shakely, our editor, for her enthusiasm and guidance, as well as all of those at Clarkson Potter who contributed their energy to this book, most notably Marysarah Quinn, Kathryn Crosby, Liana Faughnan, and Lauren Monchik. Our gratitude also goes to Drew Hodges, who in designing this work captured the project's essence; to Katherine Cowles, who understood our concept even in its earliest stages; and to Millie Martini Bratten, editor-in-chief of *Bride's,* for her thoroughly positive outlook.

We would also like to extend a special thank-you to Jonathan Adewumi, Michael Amuross, Laurie Arons, Carrie Brown, Salvador Calvano III, Chia Chin, Harriete Cole, Terrie Collymore, Phyllis Cox, Thomas Csiha, John Dolan, Vicki Dwight, Nancy Habel, Marc Joseph, Christina Kara, Amy Keith, Jenna Lyons, Jennifer McGarigle, Napata Mero, Robert Mullins, Mary Ellen Murphy, Michelle Pattee, Raja, Benita Raphan, Frannie Ruch, Polly Schoonmaker, Kate Stanley, Nancy Taylor, and Lena Youm.

introduction

Everyone knows what a wedding is all about: a woman in a long white dress, a man in a tuxedo tugging his collar, and pew after pew of family members and friends, all wondering: (a) if this radiant person known as the bride is the same girl they saw last week doing her laundry and (b) how close they'll be seated to the band.

We have all been there, we have all gotten mushy when the groom croaked out his vows, we have suffered through the best man's toast, we have danced to "We Are Family." And we have sworn that when our day came, our wedding would be different.

There is a reason why so many weddings seem to be cookie-cutter productions: planning a wedding is fun, but it is also work. In addition to making the decision to commit yourself to one person forever after and putting together what will probably be the biggest party of your life, there are families to please and placate, funds to be allocated, guest lists to be trimmed, and complex rules of etiquette to be followed. It is no wonder that so many couples, by succumbing to the pressure to do things "right," end up with the same big white wedding they have attended a dozen times before.

The weddings in this book break out of that mold. Bolstered by a strong sense of personal style and a clear vision of how they want to celebrate one of the most important events of their lives, the brides and grooms in *Real Weddings* have reinvented this most traditional of rituals. Of the hundreds of weddings we've attended, these are the ones that stand out, not for the money spent or the grand scale of the party, but because they are such personal reflections of two people, two families. These weddings are rich in personal style.

The couples in *Real Weddings* didn't plan to be part of anything as public as a book, but they did agree to let us publish their pictures and stories as examples of how a bride and groom can present themselves to the world in a new and unique way. They have dealt with budgets, nerves, family, and religious issues, and the results have been both emotionally stirring and just plain beautiful.

We hope this book will help the two of you plan a wedding that reflects your heritage, respects the sanctity of the occasion, expresses your love for each other, treats your guests to an amazing celebration, and leaves you in utter awe. And we raise a glass to all who undertake this amazing leap of faith and have the vision to make it their own.

home-inspired weddings

I

CLARE DE VILLIERS AND DERRICK MOORE DATE: JULY 5 LOCATION: PORTLAND, OREGON
CEREMONY: TRINITY EPISCOPAL CATHEDRAL MUSIC: DAVID N. JOHNSON, TRUMPET VOLUNTARY IN
D MAJOR; ANDRE CAMPRA, "RIGAUDON" READINGS: SELECTIONS FROM THE SONG OF SOLOMON;
E. E. CUMMINGS, POEM NO. 49 RECEPTION: THE HOME OF THE BRIDE'S MOTHER AND STEPFATHER
STYLE: SEMIFORMAL TIME: 4:00 P.M. CEREMONY; 5:00 P.M. RECEPTION NUMBER OF GUESTS: 120

The backyard wedding of Clare de Villiers and Derrick Moore combined three of the most magical qualities of stylish celebrations: elegance, simplicity, and fun. And while it looks like the ultimate big-money, cast-of-thousands wedding, all of the planning—and a lot of the hands-on work—was done by the bride and Felicity, her mother. This creative team jumped at the chance to pull off a once-in-a-lifetime party without spending a fortune.

THE PLANNING

From the start, this wedding focused on two givens: a ceremony in the church that the bride's family had attended for twenty years, and a backyard reception. Because the bride and groom came from the same religious background, deciding on the ceremony was easy: it would be a traditional Episcopalian wedding service. The reception, on the other hand, was a complicated production that evolved over the seven months of Clare and Derrick's engagement.

In the Pacific Northwest, where rain is a possibility at almost any time of year, planning an outdoor wedding takes a certain amount of courage. This couple chose the date—July 5—to coincide with the city's best possible weather and to be sure the family garden would be at its finest. The Fourth of July weekend was also a sentimental choice: it was the anniversary of their first date. And because they decided to marry on the Friday afternoon of a long weekend, guests were able to travel from around the country. A bonus: the church was in heavy demand for summer Saturdays, so holding the wedding on a Friday meant Clare and Derrick would have it to themselves, rather than being sandwiched between other weddings.

In choosing the style, Clare's priority was to avoid gimmicks—no Uncle Sam imagery or red-white-

Before leaving for church,
Clare gets a final hug.

and-blue color scheme. She and her mother, an avid gardener, approached the wedding as if it were a painting, thinking about the background (the green lawns, the terra-cotta tiles on the Mediterranean-style house) and the colors (almost all of the decoration would be bridal white, since the gardens were already in full bloom), and adding a few romantic embellishments, like trimming the gazebo with ribbons and replacing an old rubber swing with a hand-carved wooden one.

Logistically, Clare and Derrick's wedding was tricky to put together. The bride was an art director in New York City, 3,000 miles from home. Aside from three trips back to Portland, during which she and her mother met with caterers, florists, and other suppliers, she had to do most of the planning by phone. Early in the process, she realized that ceding certain decisions to her mother was the only way she would meet the deadline. By trusting her mother's taste and not becoming obsessed with details, she kept her sanity—and kept the planning on schedule.

Financially, Clare was lucky—her family could afford to give her a big wedding. But even the most affluent families have to set limits, and a budget was drawn up in the first weeks of the engagement. Clare managed not to exceed her limits by negotiating with vendors and by making several cost-cutting compromises without sacrificing style.

Knowing that they would have to rent every reception essential from chairs to salad forks, Clare and her mother decided against having their caterer supply everything, which can be expensive. Instead, they paid a visit to West Coast Event Productions, a large local company that supplies conventions and corporate parties. Just walking around the warehouse gave them ideas—the tall bistro tables they spotted, for example, would end up as drink tables on the dance floor. Among the items they rented were the tent, the tableware (including gold-rimmed dinner plates and dessert plates with a fruity pattern to match the cake), glassware, linens, chairs, tables, candelabra, and even votive candles.

CLOCKWISE FROM TOP LEFT: Flowers were placed strategically on the back patio; a young guest waits to toss rose petals on the bride and groom; flowers add color to the front door; more flowers accent the guest book.

For catering ideas they turned to friends, who recommended two caterers. Both came to the house to discuss their ideas for the wedding meal. "We learned that a good caterer has plenty of ideas but even more questions," says Clare. When and how would the hors d'oeuvres be passed—as soon as guests arrived? on platters? in baskets? How did they imagine the buffet would look? Where would coffee be served?

That kind of give-and-take, along with their reputation for great northwestern cooking, proved that Food in Bloom was open to Clare's ideas, schedule, and style. Cooperative in the extreme, they even agreed to incorporate several items supplied by friends of the family—smoked salmon, shellfish, local cheeses—charging only a small fee for presentation.

"Enchanting" is how Clare describes her first meeting with Polly Schoonmaker, who created the one-of-a-kind *Fantasia*-style cake. During their initial phone conversation, Clare mentioned that she wanted a different flavor for each of the three layers. Polly described twenty possibilities, and Clare narrowed them down to a handful. So in addition to looking through books of cake photos, their first face-to-face meeting included a taste test of poppy-seed cake with lemon filling, Italian ricotta mousse cake, and dark chocolate supreme cake. As they looked through Polly's portfolio, Clare pointed out details she particularly liked—the spun-sugar strawberries on one cake, the cartoonlike gum-paste hearts on another. Polly took notes, made suggestions, and afterward sent sketches and photocopies of ideas, including a picture of a wrought-iron chair whose elaborate curlicues inspired the finished product's white chocolate squiggles.

Next came the decisions about the flowers. Ironically, because Clare and her mother had such a clear idea of how they wanted the flowers to look, finding someone to do them was their biggest problem. They wanted a professional, but not someone whose ideas were too rigid. After talking with a few florists known for signature looks, Clare went in search of a more easygoing shop. At City Flowers, the staff understood that the bride and her mother wanted to take on the design themselves and were looking for a firm that would execute their plans and not intrude with ideas of their own. They worked out a simple relationship: Clare or her mother would describe the look they wanted for a particular arrangement or bouquet, and the florist would suggest several specific choices.

Clare and Derrick also learned that booking a good dance band over the Fourth of July weekend—especially with a jazz festival in town—is a challenge. A month before the wedding, they still weren't sure whether they would have to settle for a boom box and CDs. But throughout the spring and into the summer, Clare's mother continued to send them tapes of every available musical group in the city. Clare says it was plain dumb luck that led them to Soul Vaccination, a twelve-piece funk and blues band. After they listened to their tape and decided that guests with sensitive ears would have enough room to stay out of range, they signed the contract.

When Clare visited a New York stationery shop to look over the invitation options, she was taken aback at the cost. The heavy engraved invitations she wanted were a thousand dollars over her budget. She found an elegant compromise: a slightly lighter-weight paper, which also saved on postage costs, and standard ink rather than a custom-blended color. The final invitation was composed of six pieces: outer and inner envelopes, the invitation itself, the response card and envelope, and the map directing guests to the church and reception.

When it came to choosing a wedding dress, Clare faced the same challenge as many other brides: she wanted to be fairly well covered for the ceremony but a little sexy (and comfortable) during the reception. And early in their engagement, Derrick had pleaded with her not to wear a pouffy "meringue" dress.

The Vera Wang dress she ultimately fell in love with was romantic and elegant at the same time: a body-skimming silk sheath with a long side slit and a sheer back of stretch illusion. For the ceremony, opera-length gloves and a cathedral-length veil edged with satin ribbon provided some coverage; both came off once the party began. The finishing touch: a white satin stole to combat any late-night breezes.

FROM LEFT TO FAR RIGHT: After photos on the lawn, Clare and Derrick prepare to greet their guests; Derrick and the men of the wedding; African violets trimmed with ribbon; the lawn transformed into a garden party.

THE DAY

Portland's Trinity Episcopal Cathedral, the oldest church west of the Mississippi, needed very little decoration. With its bright red door, its stone arches, and a swarm of guests in their summer best, it was positively festive. Inside, several pews nearest the altar were trimmed with ivy and freesias tied with long satin ribbons to draw attention to the "wedding" part of the church. The altar was flanked by tall vases of flowers, and programs that Clare had created on her computer were placed at the end of each pew. The church choirmaster, John Strege, performed on the rare French organ.

As the groomsmen, in classic afternoon ensembles of strollers, gray vests, and four-in-hands, escorted the last guests to their seats, Clare's mother came down the aisle in a long gold sarong suit, on the arm of the senior usher. Next, the two bridesmaids entered the church in long sleeveless midnight-blue sheaths, carrying bouquets of yellow freesias and white roses mixed with blue hyacinths. The flower girl followed in a short white dress that echoed some of the details of Clare's own gown. She carried a

flower pomander on a long white loop of ribbon—the easiest kind of bouquet for a child to handle.

Finally Clare appeared on her stepfather's arm, the column of her dress framed by the cathedral-length tulle veil. She carried a hand-tied bouquet of white tulips embellished with six feet of wired ribbon. At the altar, she and Derrick faced the minister for the Celebration and Blessing of Marriage, readings, and prayers.

After the service, the couple hugged guests, posed for pictures, and were pelted with birdseed. The church bells pealed, and everyone headed to the reception, twenty minutes away.

July 5 was one of the few days that summer when the sun shone on Portland. Although thunderstorms the night before had sent the bride's mother and stepfather scurrying into the backyard to move chairs and tables, the wedding day itself was clear and bright, with only an occasional decorative cloud crossing the sky. Guests followed "Wedding Reception" signs to the family's house, a grand Italian-style mansion that neighbors call the villa. Flowers

were placed strategically: tendrils of orchids and ivy on the front door, full-blown pink peonies and white roses by the guest book, and a small forest of topiary rose trees that Clare's mother had nurtured all through the spring. (That morning the florist had filled in the bare spots by wiring on extra flowers.) Pots of pink geraniums flanked the steps leading to the front door.

Behind the house, fifteen tables were placed in two groupings on the lawn and covered with white tablecloths enlivened by African violets, an allusion to Clare's South African roots. With simple white wooden chairs, a ribbon-trimmed gazebo, and the wooden swing hung from a shade tree, the scene looked like a storybook garden party.

Cocktails and hors d'oeuvres were passed by a team of four waiters while children ran about tossing rose petals, which the bride's mother had been collecting for months and had kept fresh in plastic bags in the refrigerator.

Local specialties and some of Oregon's outstanding wines and microbrews were incorporated into the menu. Clare wanted to serve Pacific Rim cooking, but she also wanted to make sure everyone had enough to eat. She decided to pass elaborate hors d'oeuvres—which guests tend to remember most—and to keep the buffet dishes fairly simple. Surrounding the food platters was a garland of green pittosporum, ferns, and boxwood; the table was also decorated with fresh pears, peaches, and apples as well as Clare's favorite flowers—scabiosas, sweet peas, and delphiniums.

Except at the head table, the casual, no-place-cards, no-seating-plan reception meant guests could sit wherever they liked, moving to the buffet at their leisure and mingling table to table. Waiters circulated around the lawns, replenishing wine.

After coffee was served, the guests were ushered inside to the dining room, where the wedding cake sat on a platter painted with gold-leaf squiggles. Although the band winged it when it came to the first dance ("I can't even remember if we actually requested anything at all," says Clare), the bride and groom swayed and dipped with grace, after which the dance floor exploded with music. As daylight dimmed, waiters moved from table to table lighting votive candles; elaborate candelabra helped illuminate the bar. Five hours and a lot of Pinot Noir later—shortly before midnight—the last guests called it a night.

on backyard weddings:

› A HOME WEDDING IS THE MOST COMPLICATED OF ALL, AND IT ISN'T NECESSARILY LESS EXPENSIVE THAN ONE HELD IN A HOTEL OR RESTAURANT. KEEP IN MIND THAT YOU'LL HAVE TO RENT EVERYTHING FROM CHAIRS TO ICE BUCKETS.

› THE ONE THING YOU CAN'T CONTROL IS THE WEATHER—ALWAYS HAVE AN ALTERNATE INDOOR PLAN. YOU CAN RENT A TENT WITH A RAISED PLATFORM AND HAVE IT SET UP AT LEAST A DAY BEFORE THE WEDDING, TO PREVENT RAIN FROM SOAKING THE GROUND, OR YOU CAN CLEAR FURNITURE OUT OF THE HOUSE SO YOUR GUESTS WON'T BE BUMPING INTO CHAIRS.

› WE HIGHLY RECOMMEND HIRING A WEDDING CONSULTANT, IF NOT TO DO THE LONG-TERM PLANNING, AT LEAST TO TAKE CARE OF DETAILS ON THE DAY ITSELF. HE OR SHE WILL BE ABLE TO TELL THE BAND WHERE TO SET UP AND WHEN TO START PLAYING, ORCHESTRATE THE MAJOR MOMENTS (THE TOASTS, THE FIRST DANCE, THE CAKE-CUTTING), AND DEAL WITH EMERGENCIES, LIKE A MISSING CASE OF CHAMPAGNE.

› MAKE SURE YOU HAVE ENOUGH PARKING (AND PERMITS, IF NEEDED), ADEQUATE BATHROOM FACILITIES, AND ENOUGH LIGHTING SO THAT YOUR GUESTS WON'T BE TRIPPING OVER THE SPRINKLERS.

› ALERT THE POLICE IF YOU THINK THERE COULD BE A TRAFFIC PROBLEM.

› TELL YOUR NEIGHBORS ABOUT THE WEDDING FAR IN ADVANCE, SO THEY WON'T PLAN A GARAGE SALE OR MAJOR LAWN WORK ON THAT DAY.

› POST SIGNS EVERYWHERE TO GUIDE GUESTS TO THE SITE. MAKE SURE THE SIGNS ARE BIG ENOUGH TO READ FROM A MOVING CAR.

› DON'T BURDEN YOURSELF WITH TOO MANY HOUSEGUESTS. ARRANGING FOR SOMEONE TO PROVIDE BREAKFAST FOR A CROWD IS THE LAST THING YOU NEED WHEN YOU ARE DIRECTING A FLORIST, NEGOTI-ATING WITH A CATERER, AND TRYING TO GET YOUR MAKEUP DONE.

› *PHOTO TIP:* FOR A BACKYARD WEDDING YOU CAN SAVE A LOT OF TIME BY HAVING YOUR FAMILY PIC-TURES TAKEN AT HOME BEFORE THE CEREMONY. TALK WITH YOUR PHOTOGRAPHER ABOUT SCHEDULING AN EXTRA HOUR FOR FORMAL PORTRAITS PRIOR TO LEAVING FOR THE CHURCH.

TIPS

baker

POLLY SCHOONMAKER

the professionals

NUMBER OF YEARS IN BUSINESS: Ten, five on her own.

WHAT I LOVE ABOUT DOING WEDDINGS: Even though I'm dealing only with one small part of their whole wedding, meeting the couple and learning about their relationship—and you really do get to know a lot about them—is a wonderful process. There is something about making even this small dream come true, helping them realize their vision, that is incredibly rewarding.

HOW I WORK WITH A CLIENT: Cakes are a combination of looks and taste, so the first step is for a couple to start paging through my portfolios while I listen and take notes. More often than not, the guy will be the one with the majority of ideas and opinions, probably because the cake is a fairly architectural part of the wedding and the most "unbridal" element of the planning. Some clients make little drawings; others just talk about all sorts of noncakey stuff—the band they're hiring, the kind of dress the bride will wear.

It is really helpful for me to see the wedding invitation. One time I was able to use lines from two eighteenth-century love letters that appeared on the invitation to decorate a fondant ribbon, and then I made a heart-shaped locket out of white chocolate.

Next, we eat cake—usually five different flavors that I have chosen according to the season of the wedding. For autumn, I might prepare a caramel espresso mousse cake and another made of Oregon chai [tea]. Summer would mean something with berries. Couples almost never get more than a bite of their actual wedding cake, so I really load them up at this point. I also ask about the rest of the menu, so I can balance the flavors and the overall look of the wedding.

At the end of the meeting I'll show them a few sketches and get feedback so that I can go home and do a few drawings in color, which I then send off to the couple. I've noticed that instead of saving the top layer of the cake, a lot of people save my drawings and even frame them.

WORKING WITHIN A BUDGET: Most couples opt for a three-tier cake, which can feed 150. If a client needs to cut costs, I always suggest keeping it simple but elegant—doing something very small but special and supplementing it with undecorated cakes in the same flavors as the primary cake. You can also stick with just one flavor, instead of having each layer a different kind of cake. Another way to save money is by having a friend pick up the cake on the day of the wedding rather than asking me to deliver it.

SIGNATURE STYLE: When I got into this business, I wanted to take the idea of a wedding cake and strip it of all the Victorian froufrou, making something that is fairly tailored and contemporary. Basically, I clean up all the baroque stuff and make the cake classical yet modern. I'm also known for some pretty whimsical designs, like the cake I did for a Halloween wedding, with a tiny haunted house perched on top, complete with crooked windows and shutters.

ONE FAVORITE CAKE: For a picnic-style summer wedding, I took inspiration from a 1950s tablecloth. I painted cherries, peaches, and bows on fondant, then cut them out and applied them to the three layers to look like a quilt.

MY WEDDING PHILOSOPHY: The cake is the one part of a wedding that can be completely about the couple. I say, "Go for it."

FIVE THINGS TO TELL YOUR BAKER

1. The basics: when, where, how many guests, the overall budget, and how you heard about her—a picture in a magazine, for example, or a friend's wedding.
2. Your wedding style.
3. Your favorite foods, fruits, and flavors.
4. Any design element that is significant to the wedding—a dress detail, an unusual pattern on the groom's bow tie, the rings, or the invitation.
5. Your occupations, how you met, and what you do as a couple for fun.

FIVE THINGS TO ASK YOUR BAKER

1. Her price range—that is, the average cost of one of her cakes.
2. Where you can see her work or when you can meet to look through her books.
3. What styles she employs and what flavors she offers.
4. When she will be available and how far in advance you need to book her. The most popular bakers will be busy during most of the wedding season, so it's a good idea to have a preliminary conversation a year in advance.
5. How the cake will be transported to the wedding and how it will be set up. Also, if your baker will be using her own plate or platter, you'll need to arrange for it to be returned to her.

french twist

ERICA LENNARD AND DENIS COLOMB **DATE:** JULY 14 **LOCATION:** SAINT-MARC-JAUMEGARDE,

FRANCE **CEREMONY:** TOWN HALL AND VILLAGE CHAPEL **MUSIC:** SITAR SOLOIST **READINGS:**

PASSAGES FROM THE OLD TESTAMENT **RECEPTION:** THE *DOMAINE* (ESTATE) OF THE GROOM'S

FAMILY **STYLE:** ECLECTIC **TIME:** 3:30 P.M. CIVIL CEREMONY; 4:00 P.M. RELIGIOUS CEREMONY;

7:00 P.M. RECEPTION **NUMBER OF GUESTS:** 200

ERICA + DENIS

JULY 14

No one ever said the bride couldn't wear mauve, the groom couldn't wear pink, and the menu cards couldn't be orange. This highly individualistic couple—Erica Lennard is an American photographer based in Paris, and Denis Colomb is a French architect and designer—married at the groom's family estate in the south of France. It was a celebration of the couple, their passions, and their international cast of friends.

THE PLANNING

"We got married to have the party," says Erica, who never imagined herself as a traditional bride—or any bride, for that matter. But falling in love with Denis, a man whose network of creative friends fully complemented her own wide circle of talent, inspired the wedding that would surprise and delight two hundred guests from around the world. Indeed, upon receiving news of the wedding's location—the vast *domaine* of the groom's family, five kilometers outside Aix-en-Provence in the south of France—almost every one of the prospective guests said yes.

For the convenience of their guests, the couple chose Bastille Day—July 14. Because it is a long weekend in France, they felt it would give their local friends several days to relax with and get to know the people coming from overseas. The catch was persuading the mayor, who would perform the civil ceremony, and the priest, who would officiate during the religious rites, to give up a portion of their holiday weekend. After they had agreed (the sheer magnitude of the event helped clinch the deal), the couple had seven months in which to put together this elaborate party.

Erica's bouquet combines traditional roses with the surprise of berries.

It would be difficult to imagine a couple with more distinctive tastes. Both have traveled the world and are famous among their friends for personal style (the bride is known for her exotic wardrobe; the groom is one of the better-dressed men in France). Decades of work with designers, stylists, and florists meant that their wedding would be orchestrated down to the last rosebud.

Although their friends were the centerpiece of this celebration, with events planned to bring them together throughout the weekend, the location of the wedding was very much a matter of family tradition. Unlike the bride's family, who had relocated many times in the United States, the groom's family was long established in their small Provençal town and had celebrated many weddings in the local chapel. His parents had been married there, as had his sister and brother. Partly because of their different religions (Erica is Jewish; Denis is Catholic), the bride originally assumed they would have a simple civil ceremony. But sentiment, along with the young local priest's focus on spirituality rather than strict dogma, convinced her that a chapel service would be comfortable and moving.

The U.S. Department of Health was partly responsible for the style of the reception. At first, the couple planned for the entire wedding to take place in India, where they had traveled extensively. A close friend was busy arranging everything from Erica's wedding sari to the groom's traditional entrance on elephant, when a health warning, issued several weeks after the invitations were sent, necessitated an immediate change of venue. Not to be dissuaded, the couple decided to incorporate pieces of their "first" wedding into the French festivities—primarily in the design, music, and clothing.

Having coped with a bride's ultimate nightmare—moving the entire wedding to another continent—the couple threw themselves into the planning, spending much of February, March, and April in the town where they would marry. Money wasn't a big problem, although they were determined not to spend a fortune, but the logistics were complex. The first part of the planning involved notifying the guests about the change of venue and reserving the one hundred hotel rooms they would need for those traveling from abroad. Finding accommodations in high season, in many different price ranges, and without a confirmed guest list was a major challenge. Erica and Denis personally visited the individual properties to secure the necessary rooms, and they promised that every hotel would have a confirmation list a month before the wedding.

The second planning hurdle arose from the reception site: the groom's family estate, though grand, needed major repairs. Home weddings generally call for some minor refurbishing, but in this case the couple decided to have the grounds completely relandscaped, creating a custom-made space for the party.

In terms of food and drink, the location dictated all. "A simple, good Provençal meal" was what Denis and Erica wanted—fish from the Mediterranean, olive oil from the surrounding hills, vegetables from nearby gardens. The champagne would come from the vineyards of a family the bride had met in Paris, and the Côte de Provence wine was produced on Denis's family property. Friends who owned more substantial vineyards donated the bottles; the groom's nephews bottled it; and a friend of the couple designed the labels, featuring a sketch of the estate.

The groom's parents, who wanted to be involved in the food planning, suggested the *traiteur*—caterer—who had done the wedding of Denis's sister. The couple tasted a sample dinner, and the caterer declared that in addition to the traditional *corne d'abondance*—a horn of plenty filled with caramel-covered puff pastries—he would also contribute a special surprise.

Carrying out the Indian theme, the bride and groom decided their wedding should feature Indian music for the ceremony and cocktails, followed by contemporary dance tunes. Searching for a sitar player in Provence was one of the more challenging aspects of planning, but after the couple put out the word, friends suggested a concert-caliber sitarist whom they persuaded to play for their wedding by touting the superb chapel acoustics. For the dancing, they interviewed local DJs until they found one who was happy to stay pretty much with their play list—all their favorite music from the last ten years.

Most brides agonize over color schemes and tablecloths, but Erica's main concern was relandscaping a series of terraced gar-

CLOCKWISE FROM TOP LEFT: Erica holding a bouquet of roses and berries; the parish priest; officiating at the civil ceremony, Mayor Rippert du Prignon; a tiny attendant outfitted in an embroidered Indian dress; the village chapel, where two generations of Colombs have married.

FROM LEFT TO FAR RIGHT: The bride and groom, after the ceremony; the sitar player outside a Moroccan tent; a sari-clad guest; "Use the Ashtrays, Please"; one of Erica's attendants.

dens that had been neglected for decades. One of the first calls the couple made was to Alain David Idoux, a friend renowned for his garden designs, who set about chopping down trees and resetting a stone stairway. Also key to the plan was Roberto Bergero, an Argentinean decorator based in Paris. He embellished the pool area with dozens of throw pillows covered in a vibrant mix of Provençal and Indian fabrics; local friends contributed a dramatic black-and-white Moroccan tent.

All of the written elements of the wedding—the invitations, wine labels, place cards, and the long-weekend program—were drawn by Nicole Pibeaut, an artist friend of the couple. The charming and informal invitations, which were photocopied on bright orange paper, sent guests an immediate message about the style of the event.

While the groom bought his wedding outfit immediately after announcing their engagement (vest, coat, pants, tie, and shoes came from Paul Smith in Paris), Erica put off thinking about her clothes until spring. Although she didn't want a traditional bridal gown, the wedding sari she had originally planned to wear seemed a little too unconventional for the new site. A pale mauve Galliano jacket she found in Paris was the first part of the solution. With kimono-style sleeves lined in Indian fabric and an eighteenth-century tail, in the words of the bride, "It brought together lots of different worlds." Friends Isaac Mizrahi and his associate, Nina, picked out what they claimed would be the perfect piece to finish her ensemble. Erica was delighted with the white taffeta "fairy princess" skirt, a fantasy element she would never have bought herself. The gold-threaded silk shawl from India, which she carried over one arm, served a dual purpose: in addition to introducing another element of their original wedding site, the priest held it over the couple during the church ceremony as a huppahlike canopy.

A leaf-trimmed statue anchors the seating list.

THE DAY

With a policeman on horseback directing traffic, guests first assembled in the town hall. In France, all couples must marry in a civil ceremony, even if they will also have a religious service. Erica and Denis were fortunate that this was the first wedding presided over by Rippert du Prignon, the town's new mayor. The novelty of the occasion inspired him to deliver a very personal speech, in both French and English, which focused on the couple's travels and relationship. Instead of a standard wedding party, eight friends acted as witnesses, probably the largest such group in the history of civil ceremonies. After the vows were declared and papers signed, everyone walked next door to the small honey-colored chapel, which had been decorated with pots of lavender and white roses. The sitar player performed as guests took their seats.

Three little girls, all daughters of friends, took the place of bridesmaids during the religious ceremony. Erica outfitted her attendants in brilliant embroidered dresses she had found in India; since Roberto had run out of time, the mother of one of the girls found a local florist to make their coronets of fresh roses. Entering with his mother, Denis wore a gray tailcoat, bright green vest, and pink four-in-hand. Erica, on her father's arm, carried a bouquet of pale pink roses and deep purple berries.

In deference to Erica's Jewish background, the priest allowed the couple to choose readings exclusively from the Old Testament, which were read in French, English, and Hebrew. Following the vows, the sitarist gave a minirecital, after which friends and family showered the couple with rice and departed to prepare for the evening reception.

The bride and groom—and many of their guests—changed their outfits for the party. Erica donned her original wedding sari and a kimono; Denis wore a black satin-finish Helmut Lang tuxedo that he had bought on a whim, not sure when or if he would ever need it. At the groom's *domaine*, guests passed under trellises of olive branches and rosemary that Alain had cut from the property. As a safe alternative to candles, Japanese paper lanterns lit the pathway from the parking lot, ending at the swimming pool, which was surrounded by dozens of pillows where guests could recline during the casual cocktail hour. The sitar player set up shop beside the Moroccan tent while guests enjoyed a traditional Provençal spread.

Dinner was served at tables both round and rectangular. The metal chairs, painted green and orange, were from the town hall—Denis had remembered seeing them once and asked the mayor to lend them for the evening. The ceramic centerpieces—reproductions of eighteenth-century vessels, borrowed from friends who own a decorating shop in Paris—were filled with five hundred white roses; tables were covered with tangerine-colored cloths.

Every wedding needs a small disaster, and this one struck during the first course, when Erica noticed that the fish, which was to be a sautéed mullet served with herbes de Provence, was being served raw. "Some Americans were trying to cut into it, thinking it was Provençal sushi," she relates with horror. Denis ran into the kitchen to alert the caterer, and the rest of the meal went off without a hitch. Erica says she learned a big lesson about entertaining: the most important elements are the setting, having plenty of good wine, and being surrounded by people you care about.

Every wedding also has a surprise, and this had two. The first one was the caterer's dessert fantasy: melons, plums, grapes, lemons, and other fruits assembled into an edible man—"Way, *way* over the top" is how Erica describes it. The second came in the form of a dancer who, to the delight of both bride and groom, was hired by friends to perform a traditional Indian wedding dance. Afterward the DJ turned up the volume and two hundred thoroughly dazzled guests danced until 4:00 A.M.

FROM LEFT TO FAR RIGHT: The "way-over-the-top" edible man; orange menu cards and brilliant vegetables add color to the dinner tables; one of Erica's attendants ascending a staircase.

FROM LEFT TO RIGHT: Erica and Denis in their post-ceremony finery; the second surprise of the evening, a traditional Indian wedding dance.

on weddings abroad:

› RESEARCH RESIDENCY REQUIREMENTS WELL IN ADVANCE. BECAUSE DENIS IS FRENCH, HE AND ERICA WERE ABLE TO AVOID THE TWO-MONTH RESIDENCY REQUIREMENT STIPULATED FOR FOREIGN COUPLES MARRYING IN FRANCE. MAKE SURE YOU CAN SATISFY THE LOCAL AUTHORITIES.

› START THE PAPERWORK EARLY. MANY COUNTRIES REQUIRE DOCUMENTS TO BE SUBMITTED BOTH IN ENGLISH AND IN THE LOCAL LANGUAGE. GETTING THE PROPER LICENSE MAY MEAN ARRIVING AT YOUR WEDDING DESTINATION MANY DAYS—IN SOME CASES, OVER A WEEK—IN ADVANCE.

› MAKE SURE THE KEY PEOPLE ON YOUR INVITATION LIST, ESPECIALLY FAMILY AND ATTENDANTS, ARE AWARE WELL AHEAD OF TIME OF THE TRAVEL AND COST COMMITMENT. MOST PEOPLE WILL NEED TO PLAN A VACATION AROUND YOUR WEDDING, SO TAKE CARE TO GIVE EVERYONE PLENTY OF NOTICE.

› BE PREPARED TO ACT AS AN UNOFFICIAL TRAVEL AGENT. GUESTS WILL DEPEND ON YOU FOR HOTEL RECOMMENDATIONS AND PERHAPS RESERVATIONS AS WELL AS GENERAL GUIDANCE ON TRAVEL TO THE WEDDING. ARRANGING BULK RATES THROUGH HOTELS AND AIRLINES WILL MEAN AN APPRECIATIVE WEDDING PARTY—AND ONE THAT WILL SHOW UP.

› IF MANY OF YOUR INVITED GUESTS ARE UNABLE TO ATTEND, HAVE A POST-WEDDING CELEBRATION ON YOUR HOME TURF. BE SURE TO BRING PICTURES AND PERHAPS A VIDEO AS WELL.

› UNLESS YOU CAN PERSONALLY SPEND A GOOD DEAL OF TIME AT THE SITE PRIOR TO THE WEDDING, SECURE A LOCAL CONSULTANT OR CONTACT WHO HAS VIRTUAL POWER OF ATTORNEY.

› TAKE ADVANTAGE OF LOCAL TRADITIONS—THE MUSIC, FOOD, AND CLOTHES. A WOMAN IN FULL WESTERN BRIDAL REGALIA IN SOME FAR-FLUNG LOCATION IS GOING TO LOOK AS IF SHE TOOK A WRONG TURN ON THE WAY TO THE CHAPEL. ONCE YOU HAVE DECIDED TO MARRY ON FOREIGN SOIL, EMBRACE THE PLACE.

› *PHOTO TIP:* IF YOU ARE USING AN AMERICAN PHOTOGRAPHER, LET HIM OR HER KNOW OF ANY FOREIGN WEDDING CUSTOMS YOU WANT DOCUMENTED; SIMILARLY, YOU WILL NEED TO FILL A FOREIGN PHOTOGRAPHER IN ON THE SIGNIFICANT AMERICAN TRADITIONS HE OR SHE SHOULD RECORD.

TIPS

KRISTINA + ROBERT

FEB 28

KRISTINA LLOYD AND ROBERT SAMPLE **DATE:** FEBRUARY 28 **LOCATION:** WELLINGTON, FLORIDA **CEREMONY AND RECEPTION:** THE HOME OF THE BRIDE'S PARENTS **READINGS:** SONG OF SOLOMON, FIRST LETTER TO THE CORINTHIANS, 1–13 **STYLE:** SEMIFORMAL **TIME:** 5:00 P.M. CEREMONY; 5:30 P.M. RECEPTION **NUMBER OF GUESTS:** 200

The Scot who invented the game of golf couldn't have foreseen how he would facilitate a romance at the close of the twentieth century. And yet several centuries later, his experiments with a small white ball would bring together Kristina Lloyd and Robert Sample, a pair of sports-driven people, for a remarkable wedding just off the seventh tee.

THE PLANNING

Kristina Lloyd was applying for a job in a Florida-based golf company owned by Jack Nicklaus when her interviewer asked a fellow employee, Robert Sample, to join them. Aside from an exchange of telephone numbers, nothing of a personal nature happened. Then a year later, she called Rob to request a Nicklaus autograph for an auction, and they decided to get together—on New Year's Eve. A year after that date, he escorted her to the spot where they had first kissed, and he proposed.

Rob's imminent departure for a new position in Singapore put the wedding plans into motion immediately. After agreeing on a location (the Palm Beach home Kristina's parents were in the process of building) and setting a date (February of the following year), Kristina resigned from her job and joined her fiancé in the Far East. "I'm a homebody, but I felt we needed to spend more time together before we got married," she explains. Kristina left the planning in the hands of her mother and sister Katy—"the most creative people you can imagine"—and flew in for critical meetings.

Because her parents were in the midst of building their dream house on a Palm Beach golf course, Kristina's biggest question regarding the wedding was whether or not she would have to equip the guests with hard hats. The bride credits her mother with handling the stress with aplomb. "She never skipped a beat, not even when people would go by on their golf carts and say, 'There's no way that house is going to be ready in time.'" Blithely, in between meetings with the architect and landscaper, Kristina's mother, Karen, started making phone calls.

A handmade jacket awaits the ring bearer.

FROM LEFT TO RIGHT: The ring bearer, sans ring pillow, encourages a flower girl; the bride and groom following the ceremony; Kristina and her father-turned-ring-bearer.

The new house's architectural style—country French—inspired the wedding dinner. The family had been to several parties provisioned by Palm Beach Catering, who suggested a Provençal menu. The dream cake popped out of the pages of a magazine, and she gave a picture of it to Sweet Tiers, a local bakery, along with a request to copy it in ivory and white, to match the color scheme.

The flowers and decoration were a bit trickier, since Kristina and her mother were long admirers of Scott Snyder, a former florist who now works in interior design. Call it sheer persuasiveness, but they were able to convince Scott to take on one of only two parties he would do that year. Along with plenty of ivories and whites, the color scheme would be augmented with lavender, a staple of the southern French countryside. There were several areas to decorate: the aisle leading to the lily pond where the ceremony would take place; the reception tent; and the exterior of the little coach house that guests would see when they arrived.

Kristina's forward-thinking parents had saved several tall stands topped with wire baskets that they had used to decorate the wedding of their daughter Katy years earlier. This time, they decided to fill them with white French tulips and use them to line the ceremony aisle. Twin rows of potted orange trees would guide the guests into the tent. Decorative lettuces were planned to augment the white tulip centerpieces; the bride's mother was taking responsibility for filling the house with orchids and hyacinths. The most romantic touch of the day would be the heart-shaped wreath commissioned to hang on the coach house. Inspired by scent, Kristina wanted to carry gardenias; she asked the two bridesmaids—her sisters—to pick their own bouquets, and she ordered a clutch of peonies for one, cream-colored roses for the other.

Kristina also trusted the music to her family. A friend of her parents suggested an eight-piece New York band led by Denny LeRoux, whose orchestra specialized in a variety of popular music that could get several generations on the dance floor. Meanwhile, the bride and groom took dance lessons in Singapore. When she arrived in Florida before the wedding, Denny and Kristina established a phone relationship. "We would get on the phone, and

he'd sing our first dance, 'Always,' and I'd try to figure out how we would move to it," says Kristina. She crossed her fingers and practiced, solo.

Katy, an artist, was the talent behind the one-of-a-kind invitation, a box that contained not only the invitation but also several objects that had personal meaning to the couple: a golf ball (naturally); a horse ribbon (Kristina had been a competitor since she was a teenager); and loose lavender, to suggest the Provençal theme. Katy found a packager to manufacture the box, and when the bride flew home, she and her sister spent twenty-four hours assembling the pieces. Kristina says, "It was one long night."

Katy's background was also helpful when it came to her sister's wedding gown—she had worked for Geoffrey Beene, and after Kristina complained that she could not find a dress she loved, they started looking through the Beene archives. While he had never offered a bridal collection, they found a dress he had designed eight years before, cut almost like a tuxedo, with a white piqué top, perfect for a garden wedding. Finding the bridesmaids' dresses was even easier. After rejecting several of Katy's ideas that involved "far-out fabrics," Kristina walked into the Geoffrey Beene showroom, spotted a dress on a mannequin, and said, "That's the one." The strapless gowns featured silver-gray bodices with pink buttons and mocha-colored skirts. Katy designed the clothes for the children of the wedding: the two flower girls were outfitted in tan dresses with white rickrack-trimmed bibs and star-shaped buttons, details that were echoed in the ring bearer's French-inspired blouse and trousers.

The men's uniforms were navy blazers and ivory pants, along with Hermès ties in a monkey-and-alligator pattern. "My mother had gotten one for my father that Christmas," says Kristina, "and it turns out it was the company's most popular pattern that year." She and her mother spent a good bit of time on the telephone trying to track down an additional seven. Eventually several were spotted in Singapore, and the rest were shipped from stores across the U.S.

THE DAY

On the morning of the wedding the Lloyds' new house, into which they had moved exactly forty-three days earlier, was a busy place. Kristina's mother was arranging flowers inside the house, children were swimming in the pool, and Katy was setting up the place cards (she had done the calligraphy herself). The day before, Sperry Tents had erected the custom-made oval-shaped structure between the guest quarters and main house ("We were lucky that they wanted an extra tent for their inventory," says Kristina), and the florist was filling it with an aisle of orange trees decorated with miniature white lights. Meanwhile, the bride got a massage,

sat still while having her hair and makeup done, and burst into tears when a bouquet arrived from Rob, along with a love letter. After that, as she relates, "Things got going really fast."

Despite a bizarre weather system that almost made the groom late for his own wedding ("He was driving from another town, and it was raining so hard he had to pull off to the side of the road," says Kristina), the Lloyds decided at noon to hold the ceremony outside by the lily pond. Arriving guests were directed to an empty lot near the house, owned by a friend of the family who had landscaped the area just for the wedding day. Seated on rows

FROM FAR LEFT TO RIGHT: The ready-for-action ring bearer; vows beside the lily pond; a heart-shaped wreath on the carriage house; the custom-made tent; bride and attendants in Geoffrey Beene; coaxing a flower girl.

of plain white folding chairs, they watched the sun wash through a dramatic display of clouds, the only evidence that tornadoes were touching down just eight miles away.

Kristina's sisters appeared, followed by the children. The nieces of the bride and groom played their parts perfectly, scattering white rose petals along the aisle, the sight of which almost brought Kristina to tears once again. Her mood lightened up immediately when she realized the ring bearer was making his own way down the aisle, chatting up the flower girls, but without the ring pillow. So as "Here Comes the Bride" swelled and her father took her arm, Mr. Lloyd grabbed the ring pillow, tucked it under his arm, and marched into the sunlight.

The Protestant ceremony was about as relaxed as a wedding ceremony can be. The kids sat on the grass; at one point, a pair of equestrians rode into view. Kristina's best friend, Jennifer, and Rob's sister, Beth, gave the readings. Throughout, the bride remained calm, clear-eyed, and confident. "I felt totally involved in what I was saying. Afterward, my best friend told me that people couldn't hear Rob, but they could sure hear me."

Kristina's mother had created a knot garden where hors

CLOCKWISE FROM RIGHT: An edible, heart-shaped napkin ring; an antique basket once used in a French vineyard marks Kristina's chair; one of the all-white centerpieces; tailored sugar bows trim the cake.

Kristina

d'oeuvres were passed and French 75s enthusiastically sampled. Since the house was so new, most of the Lloyds' friends were inspecting the interior, while the children headed for the cookies arranged on a tiny table just for them, with miniature needlepoint chairs, small candelabra, and their own place cards.

After an hour of mingling, everyone entered the tent, scented by the potted orange trees that had just come into blossom. "People kept saying, 'What is that heavenly smell?'" says Kristina. Tables were topped with baskets of white tulips and edible heart-shaped napkin rings; the bride's chair was decorated with a basket her mother had found in a Paris antiques store and filled with white flowers. The wedding couple made the rounds of the tent, stopping to speak with each guest, and made it through "Always" with aplomb. In all, it was a seamless evening: a completely packed dance floor proved that Kristina's parents knew a thing or two about music; a few watery eyes were spotted when father and daughter danced to "Daddy's Little Girl." After changing into her going-away outfit (black pants and a white T-shirt) and throwing the bouquet, Kristina joined Rob, at which point they were showered with dried lavender and exited in the convertible decorated by her sisters. "When I was getting ready to leave, I kept thinking about the whole year-long process, about how it was finally real—we were married."

on tropical weddings:

› WHEN SHOPPING FOR A DRESS, LOOK FOR SOMETHING IN A FABRIC THAT BREATHES—COTTON, LINEN, OR A LIGHT LACE. A HIGH NECK AND LONG SLEEVES WILL BE UNCOMFORTABLE, AND A LONG TRAIN WILL PROBABLY WEIGH YOU DOWN.

› RESIST THE URGE TO DO ANY SERIOUS TANNING. BESIDES HAVING TO DEAL WITH STRAP MARKS, IT'S HARD TO SHOW OFF A BRIDAL GLOW UNDER DAMAGED SKIN.

› DESIGN A MENU THAT'S LIGHT ENOUGH FOR A WARM-WEATHER LOCATION BUT ALSO FEELS FESTIVE ENOUGH FOR A WEDDING.

› CHOOSE HEARTY FLOWERS FOR ANY AREA THAT WON'T BE AIR-CONDITIONED.

› *PHOTO TIP:* IF YOU'RE MARRYING OUTSIDE, HOLD THE CEREMONY EITHER EARLY OR LATE IN THE DAY. THE HARSH SUNLIGHT OF MIDDAY MAKES PEOPLE SQUINT AND ALSO CASTS UNFLATTERING SHADOWS.

the professionals

makeup artist
NANCY HABEL

NUMBER OF YEARS IN BUSINESS: Ten.

WHAT I LOVE ABOUT DOING WEDDINGS: Looking back at them afterward. Honestly, there's so much pressure on me that day itself, preparing the bride and the wedding party, that it can be a nightmare. There's so much emotion—if one little thing goes wrong, the bride may go to pieces, or I might be concerned that the groom will complain that she doesn't look like herself. So basically the part of a wedding that I like is when it's all over and I think about how great everyone looked.

HOW I WORK WITH A CLIENT: There is so much at stake on the wedding day that I always think it's a good idea to do a test run. Ideally a woman will bring me a picture of herself in which she likes how her makeup looks. Then I'll suggest some polish but not a total renovation. She can also bring pictures from magazines that feature the kind of makeup she would feel comfortable and pretty with—even a picture of a particular kind of eye makeup can help. The only thing I recommend avoiding is a whole new appearance; if you don't normally wear bright red lipstick, your wedding is not the moment to try it out.

It helps me to know what the dress is like, the location of the wedding, and the bride's personality type—if she wants to look romantic or fresh-scrubbed. After the run-through, I write down the products I used, especially the lipstick—she will want to buy an extra tube to have on hand that day.

On the wedding day I arrive at least two hours before the ceremony —or earlier if there is a large bridal party (most brides have me do the bridesmaids as well as the mother of the bride). I use a light hand with the foundation and concealer. You should not wear more than you normally do, just because it's a wedding. The idea is to get it to last; powdering with a big brush after each step really works. Next I'll curl the eyelashes and apply several coats of waterproof mascara, again powdering between coats. I often put black liquid eyeliner on the top lid, which opens the eyes and makes the lashes stand out. I never use eyeliner underneath—women don't realize how easily they cry at their own weddings.

Eye shadow is applied with an extremely light touch—when you look down, you don't want people to see a big semicircle of color. I pay a lot of attention to eyebrows. After I comb them up, I fill in any patchy spots in the arch with brow pencil. Then I apply brown eye shadow with an angled brush, and finally I add a dusting of loose powder. It sounds like a lot, but when I comb the eyebrows back into place, they look completely natural. All you see is the hair on top rather than the makeup.

A light bit of blush comes next—not to contour but just to give warmth, since you're going to be flushed anyway.

I use a lip pencil all over the mouth, so that even if you rub your lips together a lot (every bride gets nervous), you will still have some color underneath. Finally comes the lipstick, powdering between coats and blotting at the end. A glossy lipstick will just come off on the groom, so for shine I dot on a shimmery white eye shadow in the middle of the lower lip.

WORKING WITHIN A BUDGET: For my day rate I do the wedding party and the mothers—usually six to eight people—and I stay through the first hour or two of the reception to do touch-ups for the photographs. A tight budget isn't a problem—we can just scale back. I can do the bride and then leave her with a lipstick and compact to do her own repair work, and bill for a third of my day rate.

A WORD ON TANNING AND OTHER MISTAKES: Even if you think you look best with a tan, don't spend a lot of time in the sun just before the wedding. Your blood will be rushing to the surface, trying to heal your skin, and any makeup you put on will look caked and garish. Instead, use a big brush to apply a light dusting of bronzer over your cheeks, forehead, and chin. The other thing to avoid the day before the wedding is a face mask. Masks bring all the garbage underneath the skin to the surface. If you want to do a mask, give your face several days to recover. And if you're using an alpha hydroxy formula, skip it on the day of the wedding.

MY WEDDING PHILOSOPHY: Don't try for any look that's much "bigger" than the makeup you would normally wear. It's doubtful that you need false eyelashes or heavy lipstick to look your prettiest. People should focus on how beautiful you look, not on your makeup.

FIVE THINGS TO TELL YOUR MAKEUP ARTIST

1. The kind of makeup you wear daily.
2. Any allergies.
3. How many people you would like her to do—to avoid a time crunch.
4. What your dress looks like. Bring a picture or give her a detailed description. She will also need to know what kind of headpiece and hairstyle you will be wearing.
5. The basic logistics, including locations and a time line specifying when the hairstylist will arrive, when the photographer will set up the shots, and when the ceremony will start.

FIVE THINGS TO ASK YOUR MAKEUP ARTIST

1. Her fee and how many people it will cover.
2. Does she leave immediately after finishing the application, or does she stay to do touch-ups after the ceremony and during the reception?
3. What her strength is. If she specializes in evening makeup and you're having a daytime garden wedding, you should probably look elsewhere.
4. What makeup you will need to supply yourself. For sanitary reasons, most makeup artists don't like to use a communal mascara, so you may need to provide mascara for each of your attendants or ask them to bring their own. Also, after the trial run, find out what kind of lipstick to buy; you will want your own tube.
5. Whether or not she has a backup artist, in case an emergency prevents her from getting to you.

just family

PILAR CRESPI AND STEPHEN ROBERT DATE: JULY 19 LOCATION: EASTHAMPTON, NEW YORK

CEREMONY AND RECEPTION: THE GROOM'S HOME MUSIC: KENNY G, "THE WEDDING SONG"

READINGS: ELIZABETH BARRETT BROWNING'S SONNET 42 FROM *SONNETS FROM THE PORTUGUESE*;

PABLO NERUDA, "I DO NOT LOVE YOU AS IF YOU WERE SALT-ROSE, OR TOPAZ" STYLE: INFORMAL

TIME: 7:00 P.M. CEREMONY; 7:15 P.M. RECEPTION NUMBER OF GUESTS: 4

"I don't really like ceremonies," admits Pilar Crespi, who says she has been to only six weddings in her entire life. Stephen Robert, her husband, doesn't hold much with formalities, either—he proposed while they were in a plane over Kansas City. ("Of course, he did ask for a bottle of champagne.") In an example of stunning simplicity, they elected to hold their wedding in the groom's backyard, with their grown children as the only guests, on the anniversary of their first date.

THE PLANNING

Nowadays second- and third-time weddings are sometimes even grander than the original, but nothing was going to prevent Pilar and Stephen from keeping things "intimate and real." And so rather than worry about offending any member of their huge extended families, they elected to limit the guest list to their children. Not that there was anything meager about the event. From the bridal gown to the poetry readings, and from the flowers to the cake, this tiny wedding was a study in grace and personality.

The owner of a public relations firm, Pilar had been single for eleven years and was pretty sure she would stay that way. Then on a blind date she met Stephen, the chancellor of Brown University. "I knew immediately that he was the one," she said. The man in question, however, took his time, waiting three weeks to call her again and asserting to this day that his first marriage proposal was purely "conceptual." No matter. In April, while flying back from Los Angeles, he asked and they decided to wed sometime that summer, settling on the anniversary of their first date.

For Pilar and Stephen, making the wedding fun for their kids was the most important goal; the groom's daughters would be flying in from Boston and Los Angeles; the bride's son was interrupting

Pilar exudes cool in a celadon dress from Vera Wang.

a summer in Europe. "We wanted to make it exciting and thought about renting a boat and sailing everyone around the Sound; we even booked a table at a local nightclub where we thought we'd have dinner. But my son finally said, 'Why are you doing all this?' and we realized that having a family dinner at home would be the nicest possible way to celebrate."

Since the bridegroom's summer house had a staff to organize the champagne, cook the wedding dinner, and buy armloads of pure white flowers, Pilar had to handle only a few details herself. For the cake, she visited Gail Watson, a Manhattan pastry artist. Known for her charming tableaux made from sugar, Gail con-

cocted a light lemony cake topped with a miniature tree, inspired by Pilar's wedding gift to Stephen, a copper beech tree that she chose for its symbolism: growth and prosperity. "Trees, like marriages, need a lot of care," says Pilar.

Early in the summer, Pilar decided to design her own dress. She purchased yards and yards of white chiffon with pink and blue flowers. Fate halted the enterprise when the trimmings shop to which her dressmaker had taken the fabric burned to the ground. Realizing that perhaps a simpler plan was now called for, the bride picked out a duchesse satin evening dress from Vera Wang, a long column of shimmery celadon green.

CLOCKWISE FROM FAR LEFT: Post-ceremony hugs; the back porch, just hours before the wedding; bride and groom embrace; white flowers filled the house; the family dog, dressed for the occasion.

FROM LEFT TO RIGHT: Dinner for six; Gail Watson's beech cake; Pilar's bouquet was a gift from a friend.

THE DAY

The masses of white tulips, roses, and orchids being delivered were pretty much the only clue that a wedding was scheduled for that evening, as Pilar, Stephen, and their children spent a typical summer day at the beach. At three o'clock Sebastian, Pilar's son, asked her what she thought he should wear, and they went shopping. An hour before the ceremony, Stephen was playing tennis; thirty minutes before she was scheduled to be married, Pilar still hadn't had her hair or makeup done (the stylist was stuck in traffic on the Long Island Expressway and arrived with just fifteen minutes to spare). She was dressing when Sebastian finally asked who

was walking her down the aisle, and then declared that as the head of their family he would do the honors. When the judge showed up just before seven, she encountered a surprisingly relaxed group, considering they were all late for a wedding.

Stephen, his daughters, the family dog, and the judge stood in the garden, beneath the beech tree, as mother and son approached to the melodies of a saxophone, Pilar carrying a bouquet that a dear friend had given as a present. Stephen had suggested that they each read a poem, out of sentiment as much as a desire to prolong the ceremony. Pilar began, "How do I love thee? Let me count the ways," the Elizabeth Barrett Browning poem that she says requires "complete love." Stephen followed with words from Neruda, and the judge performed the brief civil ceremony. Afterward, champagne appeared, glasses were raised, and the small party drifted toward the patio to open gifts.

What can you say about a happy family dinner? People talk, they laugh, they tell funny stories, compliment the chef, and ask for seconds of dessert. Afterward a few local friends dropped in to toast the couple with glasses of lemon liqueur. And on this July evening that, pretty much, was that. Remarks Pilar, "I don't like to have things too planned out, and our wedding was no exception. It was warm, intimate, and real, *exactly* how I expected it to be."

on an intimate wedding:

› MAKE EVERYTHING AS EXQUISITE AS POSSIBLE, BUT KEEP IT IN PROPORTION—NO CATHE-DRAL TRAINS OR FOUR-TIER CAKES.

› THIS IS ONE OCCASION FOR WHICH YOU CAN ASK EACH OF YOUR GUESTS TO PREPARE SOMETHING TO SAY, EITHER DURING THE CEREMONY OR AFTERWARD, AS A TOAST.

› DON'T SUCCUMB TO THE TEMPTATION TO INVITE MORE PEOPLE AT THE LAST MINUTE. THE REASON YOU ARE HAVING SUCH A SMALL WEDDING—WHETHER IT'S TO AVOID HURTING ANY-ONE'S FEELINGS OR TO KEEP IT "JUST FAMILY"—WILL NOT CHANGE JUST BECAUSE YOUR COLLEGE ROOMMATE IS IN TOWN.

› SMALL DOESN'T MEAN SLAPDASH. CERTAIN ELEMENTS OF A WEDDING—GETTING THE MAR-RIAGE LICENSE, FINDING AN OFFICIANT—HAVE TO BE TAKEN CARE OF WELL AHEAD OF TIME.

› *PHOTO TIP:* WHEN THERE IS NO CROWD TO BLEND INTO, A PHOTOGRAPHER CAN SEEM OBTRUSIVE. IT WILL HELP IF YOUR PHOTOGRAPHER ARRIVES EARLY TO ASSIMILATE INTO THE GROUP, AND IF SHE USES A LONG LENS, WHICH ALLOWS HER TO STAY SOME DISTANCE FROM THE SCENE.

TIPS

heritage-inspired weddings

II

african rhythms

RHONDA REED AND ELLIOT BLADES DATE: MARCH 30 LOCATION: DELRAY BEACH, FLORIDA CEREMONY AND RECEPTION: THE MORIKAMI MUSEUM AND JAPANESE GARDENS READINGS: "TODAY IS NOT JUST SUNDAY" (MODIFIED), FROM *AFRICAN-AMERICAN WEDDING READINGS;* SUSAN TAYLOR, "WHEN YOU'RE LOVING/YOU'RE IN HARMONY WITH LIFE"; I CORINTHIANS 13:4–8; CHESTER HIMES, "MAKE TIME FOR ONE ANOTHER"; ROMANS 12:9–13, 16 STYLE: DAYTIME FORMAL TIME: 11:30 A.M. CEREMONY; 12:30 P.M. RECEPTION NUMBER OF GUESTS: 50

As colleagues, they worked with vast groups of people—up to three hundred coworkers were involved on a single project. And yet, a connection ensued. A year after their first real conversation, a four-hour phone call, Elliot swept Rhonda away to a local beach, where he led her up a huge sand dune, got down on one knee, and proposed. "She kept saying, 'Stop kidding around,' and nearly knocked me down the dune," says Elliot. When reality kicked in they set about creating a wedding that reflected their heritage, with some unusual twists.

THE PLANNING

Setting the date was academic—a friend was getting married in Zimbabwe that April, and they decided to organize their honeymoon around that event. So after they announced their news in October, the wedding planning proceeded with haste—less than six months from engagement to vows.

They talked islands that first weekend—about getting married in Jamaica, or the Bahamas, or anywhere warm and tropical. But realizing that not every member on their VIP list would be able to afford such an elaborate trip—their immediate families were scattered from Alaska to New Jersey—they started thinking about southern Florida, where Elliot's sister lived. A daytime garden wedding in a "nontouristy" setting was the only parameter when Elliot started surfing the Web, eventually locating a Japanese-style museum with rolling lawns, a lake, and plenty of patios. "While we wanted an Afrocentric wedding, I liked the idea of an Eastern aesthetic as well, someplace intimate and peaceful," relates Elliot. Rhonda wasn't convinced until they paid a visit to the site in December. The museum allowed only daytime parties on Mondays, and Rhonda and Elliot bit that particular bullet

After the vows: Rhonda and Elliot revel in the moment.

with aplomb—as Rhonda explains, "We decided on an African ceremony, a Japanese garden, West Indian food, and a Monday afternoon—it made a weird kind of sense."

After locating their site, finding a caterer became their biggest concern. "It's easy if you're doing chicken," says Rhonda, "a little more complicated when you're looking for authentic Caribbean food." After interviewing half a dozen firms, they went with the Boca Raton Hotel & Club, which at the time employed two people who truly understood island cooking. The woman who was destined to put together the pieces of the wedding was Brenda Turnbull, who'd lived in the U.S. Virgin Islands for years. The chef was Michael Shirley, born in Jamaica. Together, they knew

enough about roti and Caribbean black cake to assemble as authentic a West Indian menu as south Florida had ever seen.

Although the Morikami Museum is thoroughly Asian in design, Rhonda and Elliot wanted to introduce a few African touches into the decor. Elliot asked a friend in Zimbabwe to put together a shipment of stone sculptures for the tables, as well as smaller pieces to use as favors.

For the bridal party's outfits, Rhonda and Elliot called on Jonathan Adewumi, owner of Nigerian Fabrics & Fashion in Brooklyn, New York. Known for their Afrocentric designs, Jonathan and his brother Gboyega sketched a bridal gown that was European in its cut, with gold embroidery on the hem and

train that were Ghanaian symbols for the protection of God. Elliot and his best man, Harrison, shopped for mandarin-collared tuxedos, and had Nigerian Fabrics & Fashion create vests with African embroidery. The couple also ordered golden dresses for the flower girls, who were traveling from Alaska, as well as a tunic and skirt for Rhonda's mother, who was also the matron of honor.

Since Rhonda and Elliot wanted to combine their African and American backgrounds in every aspect of the wedding, they designed invitations that featured fairly traditional wording with a tribal-inspired border. But for the music they were looking to seriously mix things up with a blend of Latin, jazz, Caribbean, and African sounds. It turned out that her funk aerobics teacher,

David Stanley, who had started his career as a DJ, was looking for a vacation. Rhonda loved his eclectic taste in music, and he liked warm weather. End of search.

Cheo Reid, Elliot's teenage nephew, was responsible for one of the most striking parts of the wedding—with three friends he formed a troupe called the Imani dancers, both to participate in the procession and to entertain the couple and their guests during cocktails.

As for readings, Rhonda relied on a childhood friend, Camilla Thomas-Jackson, who came up with the theme of love-as-garden, and began scouring sources from the Bible to *African American Wedding Readings*.

CLOCKWISE FROM TOP LEFT: Two of the Imani dancers perform for the bride and groom; Gerber daisies and graphic pottery at the head table; the African-inspired wedding cake; chef Michael Shirley attending to the Caribbean spread.

THE DAY

At the museum, as the fifty guests took their seats, the DJ played pieces from the Soweto Swing Quartet and Bobby McFerrin's "Bang! Zoom." And as a light breeze swept across the lawn, the procession of family and bridal party members, along with two male dancers carrying small spears that Elliot had found in Zimbabwe, began. The music shifted to *Dry Your Tears, Afrika,* from *Amistad,* as the two female dancers crossed the lawn scattering the aisle with rose petals. The flower girls followed and then the entire audience collapsed in a collective sob as Rhonda approached her bridegroom.

After the minister's invocation came a song from Rhonda's cousin and readings from her sister and friends. The words spoke to the singularity of the occasion: "East and West have come together, North and South, depths and heights witness this birth." Firmly clutching hands and beaming, the bridal couple listened to the minister extoll them to "strive to out-love each other."

After lunch, the best man, wearing a head mike, recruited guests onto the dance floor, the flower girls tried to get a reluctant boy to join them, and the formerly cooperative clouds bunched overhead, forcing a somewhat sped-up cake-cutting. In a gesture that single women across the country would appreciate, Rhonda decided not to throw her bouquet, instead distributing individual flowers to her sister and friends.

TIPS

on afrocentric weddings:

› BOOKSTORES, LIBRARIES, AND THE INTERNET ARE THE OBVIOUS PLACES TO BEGIN RESEARCHING AFRICAN WEDDING CUSTOMS. THE AFRICAN STUDIES DEPARTMENT AT YOUR LOCAL COLLEGE OR UNIVERSITY CAN ALSO HELP IN TRACKING DOWN APPROPRIATE READINGS.

› NOT EVERY PIECE OF THE WEDDING NEEDS TO BE PURELY AFRICAN. IN RHONDA AND ELLIOT'S CASE, THE JAPANESE BACKGROUND DIDN'T DETRACT AT ALL FROM THE AFROCENTRIC THEME; IT ADDED AN EXTRA LAYER OF ETHNIC RICHNESS.

› DON'T COUNT ON YOUR CLERGY MEMBER TO HAVE A LOT OF EXPERIENCE IN AFROCENTRIC CEREMONIES; RHONDA AND ELLIOT'S MINISTER HAD NEVER DONE ONE BEFORE. MAKE SURE YOU CLUE HIM IN UP FRONT ABOUT ANY NONTRADITIONAL ELEMENTS YOU WANT TO INCLUDE.

› *PHOTO TIP:* THE BRILLIANT COLORS OF THE CLOTHES AND DECORATIONS MAKE COLOR FILM A MUST. ALSO, BE SURE TO POINT OUT TO YOUR PHOTOGRAPHER ANY DETAILS YOU FEEL PARTICULARLY STRONG ABOUT CAPTURING—LIKE THE SYMBOLS EMBROIDERED ON YOUR TRAIN, OR EVEN THE ICING ON THE CAKE.

CAROLINE + STUART

SEPT 30

CAROLINE DICKINSON AND STUART MORRISON **DATE:** SEPTEMBER 30 **LOCATION:** NEW SHOREHAM, BLOCK ISLAND, RHODE ISLAND **CEREMONY:** HARBOR CHURCH **MUSIC:** SCHUBERT, "AVE MARIA" **RECEPTION:** THE LEWIS FARM, BLOCK ISLAND **STYLE:** FORMAL DAYTIME **TIME:** 3:00 P.M. CEREMONY; 5:00 P.M. RECEPTION **NUMBER OF GUESTS:** 150

Caroline Dickinson and her family spent their holidays on Block Island, a charmingly old-fashioned summer resort off the coast of Rhode Island; the groom had moved to the United States from Scotland. Drawing on both backgrounds, the two contingents concocted a wedding that was grand but utterly personal, rich in cultural tradition, and as beautiful as a field of heather.

THE PLANNING

"I don't think there was even a minute when we thought about having the wedding anyplace *but* Block Island," recalls Caroline, a fashion stylist with a taste for things that are simple and rugged. Similarly, introducing Stuart Morrison's Scottish heritage into the day was a given from the start. That said, the complications of holding a large formal wedding on an island where everything from the chairs to the cake had to be shipped over by ferry posed a set of logistical problems worthy of an engineer. Luckily, Caroline's father is an organizational master (he built computers for the space program), and her mother has an uncanny aptitude for detail. Knowing that Stuart's parents were eager to provide the Scottish elements, they began their planning frenzy.

The romance itself was a whirlwind—the couple met in October and became engaged in May—so it was only fitting that they also planned their wedding in a rush. They didn't want to wait an entire year for the wedding, and since the weather would turn cold early in the fall, they selected a late September day. Labor Day signals the unofficial end of the Block Island resort season, when most of the summer people close up their houses. Providentially, several close friends of the bride's parents offered the use of their homes, so guests and family could stay on the island for an extended celebration.

Though she says she went into the whole planning process thinking hers would be an untraditional party, the wedding was essentially formal, partly because of her parents. "My older sister had gotten married the previous January in a tiny ceremony in Brooklyn, and although it was lovely, my parents

In the back of a Range Rover,
Caroline and Stuart pause en route
to the farm.

had felt a little cheated," says Caroline. So they were delighted when their youngest child confided that she would love a large wedding with all the trimmings.

Two major elements set the wedding apart. The first was the contrast of a formal wedding in a rural setting: a seated dinner in the midst of a huge expanse of farmland, guests dressed in cashmere and silk, transportation via Range Rover and school bus. Like a lavish safari in the wilds of Africa, everything became more special. The other key to this wedding's style was the addition of so many Scottish details, from the sprigs of heather in the boutonnieres to the Scotch served during the cocktail hour.

During the early stages of the planning, mother and daughter visited several Victorian mansions on Block Island that were for rent. "They were huge, but the bunches of dried flowers and flocked wallpaper felt all wrong," Caroline explained. Her real dream was to hold the reception at the Lewis Farm, where her family had rented a barn during all those childhood summers. The only problem was that the owners had never made their property available for so much as a picnic, let alone a wedding for 150 people. Luckily, Caroline's mother is a persuasive and optimistic soul who took her daughter in hand and paid a visit to the owners, who said they would talk it over. A weekend later the farm was theirs.

Once the venue was booked, coping with the logistics began. Transporting the guests from the church to the reception was one of the most complicated tasks, since parking would be extremely limited at the farm. As it happened, the florist was key to solving this particular snag; together with the bride's father, he rounded up every available white Range Rover on the island to transport the wedding party, and he got in touch with the local school bus driver, who agreed to deliver the guests in shifts.

Stuart's mother took on the task of providing the formal Highland attire for the non-Scots groomsmen (the group included two of Caroline's close male friends) as well as the child attendants. The groom's friends from Scotland had their own kilts in their individual family plaids, but to create a cohesive picture, the American men also needed proper outfitting. Luckily, renting a kilt in Scotland is a lot like renting a tuxedo in the United States. The groom's mother sent instructions on how to be measured for the proper kilt length—including the distance from floor to knee—and ordered everything from socks to shoes, from jackets to the Stuart plaid kilts. She also sent Caroline a swatch of the plaid in silk taffeta for approval; it would be made into the flower girls' dresses.

Back in America, Caroline tackled the flowers. A former Hathaway shirt man, Ned Phillips had gone from modeling to landscape architecture and had recently worked with Caroline's father on his new Block Island home, Peckham Farm. Although he was best known for his large projects, Ned's reputation as a floral designer was also well established—his name came up every time the bride asked friends for recommendations. She simply showed him pictures from magazines and talked about how they could incorporate Scottish elements into the overall scheme, a feat they accomplished by placing large pots of Scottish broom (a fragrant, spiky flower) in the church and at the entrance to the tent. For the bouquets, Caroline wanted Queen Anne's lace, hydrangeas, and full oyster-colored roses. Stuart's mother was bringing the heather boutonnieres, pinned onto tartan ribbons that would match the groomsmen's kilts. For the reception, the bride envisioned her grandmother's collection of antique glass vases, old teapots, silver tureens, and porcelain bowls filled with white flowers.

After deciding that bringing a catering crew from New York was an unnecessary expense, Caroline's family turned to local possibilities. The most obvious candidate was Kurt Tonner, who had a reputation as the best provisioner in the state. Caroline calls Kurt "an artist who likes to cook" rather than the kind of caterer who is adept at organizing complex events. Kurt proved to be a good source of information, however. He suggested an outfit for tent rentals, recommended another for lighting, and even arranged to have fruitwood folding chairs shipped over from the mainland. He was particularly happy to oblige the bride's request for grills set up in the open, so that guests could watch the tuna, caught that morning, being cooked at its freshest.

The ceremony was easy to plan. The bride's mother arranged a very traditional program with the church organist and a flutist. For the recessional, one of the groom's best friends, Colin, who had flown in from Scotland with his bagpipes, played as guests exited the church.

Hiring a band for the reception was an example of how difficult island weddings can be. The big tent and seated dinner seemed to call for a grand ten-piece New York chamber orchestra, but Caroline's budget did not allow her to pay for the musicians' transportation, rooms, and meals. Ned, the florist, suggested a calypso band from Providence, which made sense from a budgetary point of view—fewer musicians, simpler transportation. The tape they sent had a "young Harry Belafonte" sound—excellent dance music, if a little unusual for the setting. But Caroline and Stuart liked the idea of mixing things up a bit, so calypso it would be.

Sticking to tradition, the bride ordered formal engraved invitations from Tiffany's with a simple navy blue border. Stuart created the invitations for the rehearsal dinner, which featured his sketches of the local lighthouse and other Block Island icons.

Caroline knows what she looks good in, and it is not ruffles and bows. At five feet eleven, she favors streamlined designs with minimal ornamentation. A woman whose taste she respected recommended, of all people, two designers in Stamford, Connecticut, who specialized in home furnishings. Another friend worked up a sketch according to the bride's instructions—a long sheath with a scoop neck, longer in back than in front—which Caroline dutifully took to her dressmakers' shop. They, in turn, created a muslin pattern that they would occasionally bring to the bride's New York office for fittings. Taking Caroline's height into consideration, the designers created a ten-foot veil that floated behind her like an elegant sail.

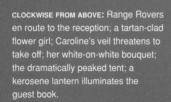

CLOCKWISE FROM ABOVE: Range Rovers en route to the reception; a tartan-clad flower girl; Caroline's veil threatens to take off; her white-on-white bouquet; the dramatically peaked tent; a kerosene lantern illuminates the guest book.

THE DAY

Caroline started her wedding day by making coffee and taking a long hike with her bridesmaids—she wanted to get some color in her cheeks. After an appointment with the local hairdresser, the bridal attendants got dressed with minimum fuss. While driving to the ceremony, Caroline spotted Stuart standing behind the church with his brother and recalls, "He looked nervous and sweaty, an absolute wreck."

Stuart wasn't the only one. As the kilted groomsmen were seating guests and distributing programs, some members of the bridal party went into panic mode. "The music started, and my twelve-year-old niece, the junior bridesmaid, started to cry because she had to walk down the aisle alone. I looked at my dad, and he looked shaky too." Nonetheless, the processional began, and the seven bridesmaids marched down the aisle in long navy dresses of knit jersey, trailed by two flower girls, Stuart's nieces, wearing tartan dresses that his mother had commissioned in Scotland. They carried baskets of flower petals; their heads were encircled with coronets of ivy and roses. Next came Stuart's nephew carrying a

tartan ring pillow and outfitted in full Highland wedding gear. Finally, Caroline appeared with her father, who had eschewed a kilt in favor of his trusty tuxedo.

Sun streamed through the stained-glass windows as Stuart's uncle delivered an eloquent service, Caroline's family minister administered the actual vows, and two groomsmen performed readings. The couple remembers the sound of people crying though. "A lot of our friends just lost it," says Caroline.

Up at the Lewis Farm, waiters passed sparkling water, champagne, and a single malt Scotch. The raw bar did a brisk business in oysters and clams, while cigars were distributed and the sunset arrived on cue. Inside the tent, votive candles created an intimate glow on tabletops, the small flames bouncing off the pitchers and vases of exuberant white flowers.

Weddings in Britain involve lots of speeches—a tradition that crossed the Atlantic with gusto. A cast of dozens rose to the occasion, including the best man, both fathers, the friend who had introduced the couple, and a guest emboldened by Scotch. Dinner

FROM FAR LEFT TO RIGHT: A single-malt Scotch keeps company with cigars; Caroline, Stuart, and a phalanx of groomsmen; the bride and groom survey the crowd.

CLOCKWISE FROM TOP LEFT: The Cupcake Café creation; the groomsmen's accoutrements included heather boutonnieres and sunglasses; family pitchers and vases were used as centerpieces; at evening's end, "Auld Lang Syne."

was finally served to a very happy, hungry crowd.

After that, "things got pretty crazy," says Caroline. Among the details that anyone can remember: the bagpiper jamming with the calypso band, Stuart and friends doing a jig, and the lemon-and-raspberry wedding cake from Manhattan's Cupcake Café. Caroline's friend John had picked up the cake at five o'clock that morning, gotten a ticket while transporting it to the island, and swore he "didn't even want a taste."

The bride was having too much fun to remember to toss the bouquet, but Stuart's Scottish contingent—including thirty-five guests who'd traveled from Britain to the ceremony—came together at the evening's end to link arms with Caroline and sing "Auld Lang Syne," the proper close to any Highland wedding.

TIPS

on island weddings:

› IT HELPS ENORMOUSLY IF YOUR KEY CONTACT HAS LIVED ON THE ISLAND FOR A LONG TIME. YOU WILL DEPEND ON HIS OR HER ADVICE ABOUT HIRING HELP, AND PEOPLE WHO LIVE IN SMALL COMMUNITIES FORM GOOD WORKING RELATIONSHIPS WITH PROFESSIONALS THEY TRUST.

› PLANNING A WEDDING FOR JUST AFTER THE HEIGHT OF VACATION SEASON WILL FREE UP RECEPTION LOCATIONS AND HOTELS, BUT ISLANDS GENERALLY GO INTO SLOW SEASON BECAUSE THE WEATHER IS SHIFTING. ON SOUTHERN ISLANDS, MARRYING AFTER EASTER MAY MEAN SWELTERING GUESTS; IN THE NORTH, MARRYING AFTER LABOR DAY WILL PROBABLY MEAN A CHILLY EVENING.

› WHETHER YOUR ISLAND IS CONNECTED TO THE MAINLAND BY FERRY, BRIDGE, OR PLANE, THIS WILL NOT BE A NORMAL COMMUTE. THE KEY MEMBERS OF THE WEDDING SHOULD PLAN TO ARRIVE ON THE ISLAND THE DAY BEFORE THE EVENT.

› SINCE THE WEDDING IS TAKING PLACE IN AN ESSENTIALLY RELAXED LOCALE, DON'T COUNT ON ANYTHING BEING DONE WITH MILITARY PRECISION. EMBRACE THE CONCEPT OF ISLAND TIME.

› *PHOTO TIP:* IF YOU MARRY ON AN ISLAND, MAKE SURE THE PHOTOGRAPHER KNOWS JUST HOW DIFFICULT IT WILL BE TO BUY FILM OR RENT EQUIPMENT AT THE LAST MINUTE. AND PROVIDE *DETAILED* DRIVING DIRECTIONS—ISLAND ROADS ARE OFTEN UNMARKED, AND YOU DON'T WANT YOUR PHOTOGRAPHER TO MISS THE FIRST DANCE.

MARIA + JEFF

OCT 4

MARIA PEREZ AND JEFF ARONS **DATE:** OCTOBER 4 **LOCATION:** CUPERTINO, CALIFORNIA

CEREMONY: SAINT JOSEPH CHURCH **MUSIC:** SCHUBERT, "AVE MARIA"; "PESCADOR DE HOMBRES";

"ALL I ASK OF YOU," FROM *PHANTOM OF THE OPERA;* WEDDING MARCH **READINGS:** CORINTHIANS

("THE GREATEST GIFT IS LOVE"); PABLO NERUDA **RECEPTION:** THE HOME OF DRS. MALCOLM AND

JUSTINE FORBES **STYLE:** INFORMAL **TIME:** 12:00 NOON CEREMONY; 1:00 P.M. RECEPTION

NUMBER OF GUESTS: 160

A taste of Mexico was transported to northern California for the wedding of Guadalajara-born Maria Perez and her American tennis-pro groom, Jeff Arons. Working with the groom's sister, Laurie Arons, who is a professional wedding planner, they put together a festive backyard reception on a shoestring.

THE PLANNING

When Jeff proposed to his Spanish tutor, Maria, they had a couple of basic considerations: combining two heritages and doing it on a budget that made Laurie Arons gulp and say, "Okay, but you are really going to have to work with me on this." That meant keeping the number of guests manageable, borrowing whatever they could, and planning a midday wedding rather than an elaborate dinner.

After two years of living together, Jeff and Maria spent one day in May going over every aspect of their dream wedding—this despite the fact that they weren't even engaged. Finally, at the end of the evening, he turned to her and said, "By the way, would you like to get married?" The first call they made was to Laurie, who listened to their plans for an outdoor reception and suggested that October would be the safest weather month; they glanced at a calendar and picked the first weekend.

Like many couples today, Maria and Jeff wanted to blend two family traditions. "I was born in Mexico and raised a Catholic, Jeff's Jewish and from California, and we both thought it would be really important to include the two cultures in the ceremony and reception," remarks Maria. So they chose a Catholic church for the service, introduced Jewish rituals into the ceremony, hoped to hold the reception at the home of a friend of the Arons family, and looked at the party as a wedding fiesta, full of the sounds and tastes of Maria's childhood.

In a tribute to her Guadalajara roots, the bride found a nine-piece mariachi band led by Francisco Ponce to welcome guests to the reception.

CLOCKWISE FROM ABOVE: Maria, her brother, and the ring bearer driving to the ceremony; a young guest inspects the flower girl's bouquet; Maria and Jeff as husband and wife; bride and groom enter the reception site; on the memory table, a picture of Jeff's early form.

To keep within their budget, they decided on an afternoon wedding so that they could serve a light meal and have several food stations. This device saves money when it comes to rentals, since not all of the guests need assigned seats; a lot of people like to talk and mingle. It also saves on flowers (fewer tables means fewer centerpieces) and even cutlery, since finger foods mean you can make do with forks alone.

"If you're going to get married on a shoestring, make sure there's a wedding coordinator in the family," says Jeff, who relied on his sister, Laurie, to put together all of the major elements of the wedding. Working with a budget that usually covers just her personal fee, Laurie pulled every string she could.

Even though the recently relandscaped garden at the Forbes home didn't need a lot of embellishment, Laurie knew that flowers were always one of the most important parts of a wedding, and she suggested hiring Clare Webber as the florist. Clare listened to Maria's request for "soft colors—pink, blue, and white," and constructed a couple of elaborate arrangements to dress up the church, bouquets of cream and yellow roses for the bride and her attendants, and charming heart-shaped topiaries for the backyard. The centerpieces were small vases of old-fashioned pink and white roses. Maria was beyond appreciative: "It's incredible how much time it takes to plan a wedding. I was so lucky to have Laurie recommend someone I could absolutely trust."

Since the food was the one detail most likely to say "fiesta," Laurie and the bride and groom were determined to find the right caterer. Bird of Paradise, a purveyor of the kind of light, healthy food Maria and Jeff like, agreed to provide the Mexican-American menu. To satisfy the Mexican contingent (many members of Maria's family were flying up from Guadalajara), there were fish and chicken fajitas, tacos, lots of salsas, and chips—finger foods that were easy to eat. To please the American crowd, they devised several pasta dishes. And to the delight of everyone, margaritas were served up in thick Mexican glasses decorated with little hand-blown cacti, and the bar was stocked with Coronita beer. Laurie chose the wines and champagne.

Maria wasn't going to be fussy about the way her wedding cake looked, but she definitely knew how she wanted it to taste—"chocolate, chocolate, chocolate." A local bakery, Cakework, did the sweet three-tier confection covered with white chocolate pearls and shavings.

The wedding wasn't just going to taste bicultural, it would sound bicultural, too. For the ceremony, Maria's piano teacher introduced her to a bilingual soloist who sang in both Spanish and English. During the first part of the reception, the bride wanted to honor her Guadalajara roots—the city is renowned as the birthplace of the mariachi band—and asked a local restaurateur for recommendations. He told her to come back and listen to a nine-piece mariachi band led by Francisco Ponce that played all the traditional tunes Maria wanted.

Dance music was another matter. Jeff is a James Taylor fan and had his heart set on the singer's rendition of "Something in the Way She Moves" for their first dance. Since it is hard for anyone but James Taylor to sound like James Taylor, Jeff decided to bring a CD. Laurie located the main band, Napata Mero and the Chocolate Kisses, who kept the guests on their feet.

The cream-colored invitations, embellished with a little pot of flowers, were simply worded, "Together with their parents, Jeffrey Arons and Maria Perez invite you to . . ."

"I don't want a big dress that looks like a house" is just about all Maria told Laurie when she headed out looking for a dress. She found her gown on the first try, at a bridal salon owned by another of Laurie's contacts, Joan Gilbert. The details were minimal—silk rosettes around the off-the-shoulder neckline, with a short train—about as uncomplicated as a bridal gown can be while still allowing Maria to look every inch a bride.

The three bridesmaids—Maria's cousin, her sister, and her language tutor, who was a childhood friend of Jeff's—were similarly lucky. Maria sent each of them a swatch of navy blue fabric and told them to buy anything they liked that was long and sleeveless. In keeping with the simple scheme of things, the groom and ushers wore blue blazers and khakis.

THE DAY

People sometimes complain about children at weddings, but Maria invited nearly every child she knew—children she had baby-sat, two flower girls, and her three-year-old nephew, who carried the rings. So while the ceremony started calmly enough, with songs in both English and Spanish, a reading from Corinthians (also done in both languages), and a poem by Pablo Neruda, it did take on a whimsical quality when the ring bearer realized that Jeff, and not he, was marrying the bride. "He kept trying to get my attention, demanding his own ring, lying down on the carpet, and making a fuss. Even the priest was smiling."

After the blessing, the couple shared the Jewish tradition of drinking from a goblet of wine; Jeff then took a glass wrapped in a handkerchief and smashed it underfoot; the shards served as symbols of their many years ahead.

After exiting the church, the bride and groom climbed into the 1931 Packard Phaeton convertible that a friend of Jeff's family had lent for the day, and acknowledging the waves and honks of other cars, drove to the Forbes residence, where long ribbons hung from two white poles to help guests find the turnoff. As they entered the reception area, the mariachi band struck up "Guadalajara," and the margaritas started to flow. Waiters circulated with hors d'oeuvres. An hour later the food stations opened, and guests dipped into ceramic bowls of salsa, munched on fajitas, and devoured the pasta.

The mariachi band played for a good two hours before Jeff announced that he was dedicating "Something in the Way She Moves" to his bride. Following the first dance, Napata Mero and the Chocolate Kisses went into gear, with three soul singers doing their Motown thing in spangly white dresses. "Everyone—and I mean *everyone*—was dancing," remembers Maria, "even the kids, my relatives from Mexico, and especially my brother. I think he danced with every single woman there."

In an inspired touch, Kathy, the bride's language tutor and attendant, had requested that all of the guests bring pictures of the couple from childhood to the present. She set up a table with an album, pens, and markers, for the guests to write down their memories and hopes for the couple. So while the cake was cut and the espresso bar opened for business, a line of guests formed to paste in photographs and do a bit of personal scribbling, creating a memento that very much summed up the cross-cultural spirit of the day.

TIPS

on bicultural weddings:

› AGREE AT THE START THAT BOTH FAMILIES AND BOTH TRADITIONS WILL BE HONORED.

› TRY TO MAKE THE WEDDING A REFLECTION OF YOU AS A COUPLE RATHER THAN AS TWO PEOPLE WITH DIVERSE BACKGROUNDS.

› TALK WITH BOTH FAMILIES UP FRONT ABOUT THE RITES OR RITUALS THAT ARE MOST IMPORTANT TO THEM. TRY TO LIMIT EACH TO THREE OR FOUR REQUESTS.

› IF THE WEDDING IS ON YOUR TERRITORY, LET YOUR FIANCÉ INTRODUCE ENOUGH OF HIS OWN TRADITIONS TO MAKE HIS FAMILY FEEL A WELCOME PART OF THE CELEBRATION, AND VICE VERSA.

› PEOPLE LOVE TO KNOW THE HISTORY OF RITUALS, PARTICULARLY IN A BICULTURAL WEDDING. YOUR PROGRAM SHOULD IDENTIFY ANY RITES OR READINGS THAT MAY BE UNFAMILIAR TO YOUR GUESTS.

› *PHOTO TIP:* MAKE SURE YOUR PHOTOGRAPHER TAKES A GROUP PHOTO OF FRIENDS AND RELA-TIVES WHO HAVE TRAVELED FROM FAR AWAY, AND POINT OUT WHICH SPECIAL CULTURAL TOUCHES —EVEN THE FOODS BEING SERVED OR DANCES—ARE IMPORTANT AND DIFFERENT. A TIME LINE WILL ALLOW HER TO CATCH EVERYTHING SIGNIFICANT.

bandleader and vocalist
NAPATA MERO

NUMBER OF YEARS IN BUSINESS: Ten. Thirty years total in the music business.

WHAT I LOVE ABOUT DOING WEDDINGS: The versatility. Because of the wide spectrum of ages you find at a wedding, I'm able to do a real range of music styles that are all part of my personality. I start with swing music, which doesn't intimidate the older set; once they're on the dance floor and feeling comfortable, we can move into the blues, and finally, toward the end of the first set, my backup singers, the Kisses, come on and we switch into high-energy music from the sixties, seventies, and eighties.

HOW I WORK WITH A CLIENT: Our first conversation is on the phone, when we determine if I'm available for the date. Then I explain how the band works, including the fact that we employ a strong visual element in our act—lots of costume changes—which is important for the guests who aren't dancing. I talk about the transition of the music, and I'm always interested in what their first dance will be. If it's something we haven't done before, I ask them to send me a recording of it several months before the wedding so we can perfect it.

The package I send off to a client includes the proposed schedule for the reception—what we'll be doing from the time guests arrive until they leave. I also send along a list of our repertoire, which is about two hundred songs, and ask the couple to mark with a star what they absolutely want to hear, which really helps me fine-tune our sets. They also receive a video and a CD, so they really know what they're getting.

WORKING WITHIN A BUDGET: Our rate is based on a minimum block of time, which is three hours. But because the members of my band are so versatile, we're able to offer clients several ways to cut costs. My keyboard player can do a piano solo during cocktails, and then we'll segue into a jazz quintet for dinner. Then I come out at the end for the dance music. It's less expensive than hiring a ten-piece dance band to play during the entire reception.

WHAT GETS EVERYONE DANCING, EVERY TIME: Aretha Franklin. It doesn't matter what the age group is, whether the bride is twenty-one or sixty-five, Aretha is the hands-down favorite.

BIGGEST PROBLEM AT WEDDINGS: The timing. At a wedding, there's no way you can control how long the dinner is going to take or how many speeches there are going to be, which largely depends on how many cocktails have been consumed. So making the transition from dinner music to dancing is sometimes a bit tricky. But frankly, once we're there, we're completely open to the bride and groom's schedule. Things take on a life of their own, and we're happy to be along for the ride.

MY WEDDING PHILOSOPHY: Most weddings are really fun, energetic, and up. My favorite moment usually comes toward the end of the evening when the bride and groom are on the dance floor, partying hard. I take a minute to wish them the best that life has to offer and to hope that the force goes with them. I assume that it does.

FIVE THINGS TO TELL A BANDLEADER

1. Your ethnic background, so we can add appropriate songs. If the couple is Jewish, we'll play the hora; if they're Greek, we'll do a special number or two.
2. If there are any religious restrictions. It won't affect our play list so much as what we wear—for example, if the women's dresses need to be a specific length.
3. Whether or not the client wants me to act as a mistress of ceremonies, making announcements.
4. If any of the parents are divorced, it helps us to know about the stepparent situation, to structure announcements and the first dance.
5. How the bride and groom see themselves during the first dance, specifically whether they want to show off a bit and dance by themselves, or if they want the bridal party to join them on the dance floor.

FIVE THINGS TO ASK A BANDLEADER

1. If their first dance is actually danceable. It's possible that their favorite piece of music is quite difficult to move to. I remember watching one couple struggle through a reggae piece—it was excruciating. I don't want to attack the couple's taste in music, but I do want them and their guests to feel comfortable.
2. How much time it will take to set up. My technicians need anywhere from three and a half to five hours to erect the sound system and lighting. Cords have to be hidden and taped; we need time for a sound check; and the musicians need time to change into their tuxedos.
3. What size stage is needed. If the space is too small for a ten-piece band, we'll do a little give-and-take to tailor the group to the site. We also need a dressing area that isn't accessible to the guests. Even a spare office will do.
4. On a technical note, how much wattage is needed. For an evening reception, we need at least three or four 20-amp outlets.
5. Whether or not the band is willing to let the couple bring in an outside person to perform a special song or to play a specific artist's CD, which they might want for their first dance. We're completely open to both.

CLAIRE + JONATHAN

DEC 20

CLAIRE MEEHAN AND JONATHAN BAILEY DATE: DECEMBER 20 LOCATION: NEW YORK CITY
CEREMONY: SAINT THOMAS CHURCH MUSIC: SELECTIONS BY BACH; JEREMIAH CLARKE, "TRUMPET
VOLUNTARY"; "JERUSALEM"; SCHUBERT, "AVE MARIA"; "TO BE A PILGRIM"; "ADESTE FIDELES"; "ONCE
IN ROYAL DAVID'S CITY"; WIEDOR, "TOCCATA" RECEPTION: ST. REGIS HOTEL STYLE: FORMAL
TIME: 5:00 P.M. CEREMONY, 6:30 P.M. RECEPTION NUMBER OF GUESTS: 220

British to the core, Jonathan Bailey had not really considered the possibility of marrying an American girl. And having grown up in Bernardsville, New Jersey, Claire Meehan had always assumed her own wedding would involve a country setting and a bunch of wild daisies. But, as they say, never say never. The New York City Christmas wedding they planned was a joyful celebration of Old World meets New.

THE PLANNING

Boldly asking to be seated next to "the most beautiful woman" at a friend's party, Jonathan was delighted with his request as he and his dinner partner, Claire, talked into the night. After their nearly two-year-long courtship, Jonathan sat down with Claire's father, Raymond Meehan, and formally requested permission to marry Claire. The wedding planning began right there, as Claire's father offered to host the event after good-naturedly voicing his primary concern: "I'll be damned if I'm not going to have a nice dinner."

Deciding that a two-week honeymoon was a big priority, Claire and Jonathan chose a date based on her law school's Christmas break. Figuring out the location was more of a stumbling block; Claire dreamed of a wedding in her rural New Jersey hometown, but the logistics were less than ideal. "We knew we'd have a lot of guests coming from England, and the idea of them driving around in snow and ice, crashing into trees—on the wrong side of the road, no less—was pretty scary." She soon realized that a Manhattan wedding would be a far better idea.

The groom's British upbringing was integral to the style of the wedding. His first concern was the ceremony, so the couple paid a visit to Father Kraus, senior curate of their parish church, Saint

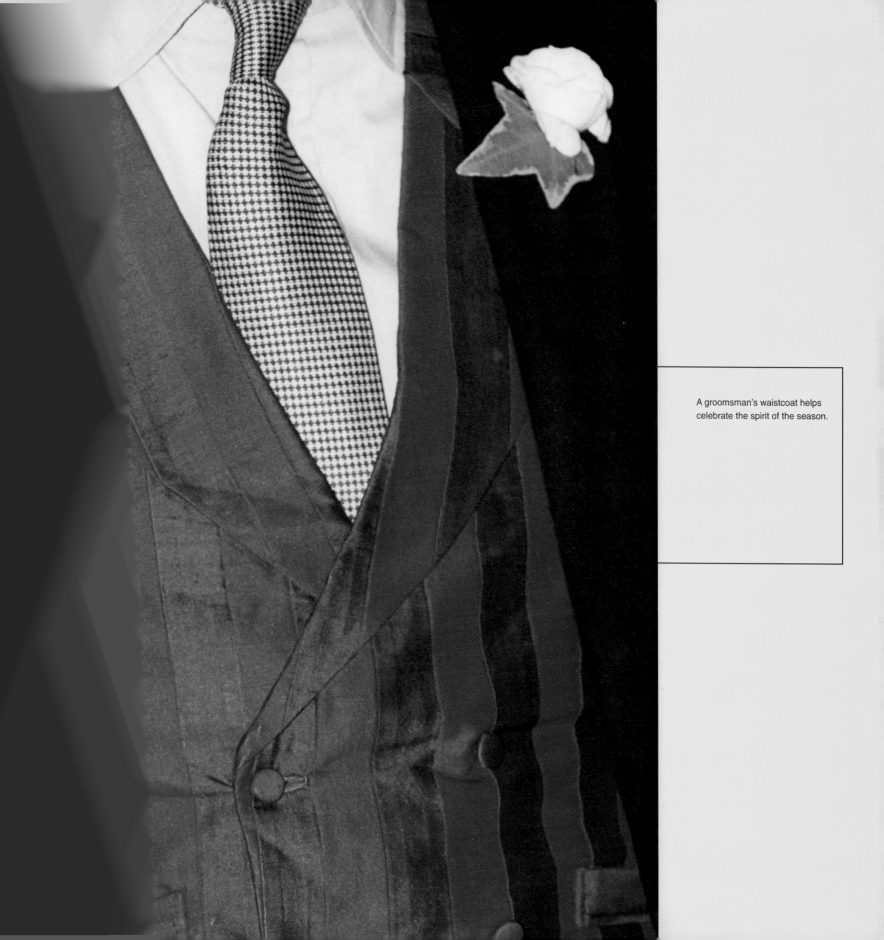

A groomsman's waistcoat helps celebrate the spirit of the season.

Thomas, a cathedral-like structure on Fifth Avenue. "Father Kraus agreed to marry us and looked forward to seeing us in church every weekend," recalls Jonathan. So in preparation of the big day, each Sunday for six months Claire and Jonathan attended Mass, often accompanied by friends who were bribed with a post-service brunch.

Location was the magic formula in choosing a reception site. Just one and a half blocks from their church, the St. Regis is known for its rooftop ballroom and excellent food. It is also one of Raymond Meehan's favorite places. Claire and Jonathan opted for cocktails and hors d'oeuvres in the second-floor Vanderbilt Rooms, followed by a seated dinner in the Roof restaurant.

Claire's mother knows and loves flowers, and worked with Stone Kelly, the Manhattan florist the bride had chosen on a friend's recommendation. Since the church would already be decorated for Christmas, they needed to add only a couple of arrangements; similarly, the St. Regis would be decked out for the holidays. So as not to compete with the surroundings, the flowers they introduced were all cream-colored: French tulips, calla lilies, roses, and peonies mixed with berries and seasonal greens for a subtle touch of holiday charm.

Claire had been searching for a dress for months and was on the brink of having something made for her when she paid one last visit to Bergdorf Goodman and found her Ulla-Maija gown, which was straight and fitted, with a tank top and a detachable cathedral train. "I didn't want to feel pouffy, but I did want some-

thing that would look dramatic going down the aisle."

The seven bridesmaids wore midnight-blue Vera Wang dresses; the flower girl, a veteran of three weddings, matched in a little girl's dress of navy blue; the page was outfitted in a miniature uniform of the Scotts Guards. In Britain, the men of the wedding party wear morning coats, no matter what time of day. So while the American contingent wore tuxedos, Jonathan's English friends were resplendent in tailcoats, striped trousers, and silk waistcoats in a kaleidoscope of colors.

"A two-month standoff," is how Claire describes the invitation debate. Jonathan wanted very English invitations—stiff, heavy things that his countrymen could prop up on their mantelpieces. Claire's father, on the other hand, wanted something American.

The ultimate compromise was smaller than Jonathan originally wanted, heavier than Claire's father thought ideal, but acceptable to everyone.

The groom's boarding school background exhibited itself most profoundly in the choice of ceremony music. Jonathan micromanaged the selections, beginning with thirty minutes of bell ringing outside the church while the organist played selections by Bach.

His heritage even showed up in the reception desserts: Claire engaged Gail Watson to prepare both a four-tier bride's cake and the traditional English groom's cake. Claire's was lemon poppyseed with raspberry mousse filling, frosted white and decorated with sugar holly leaves, bows, and flowers. Jonathan's cakes were small boxes of "the best fruitcake" they'd ever eaten.

CLOCKWISE FROM TOP LEFT: A groomsman's waistcoat; the march down Fifth Avenue; a bridesmaid; Claire looking radiant; guests mingling during the cocktail hour; the child attendants, waiting for their cue.

THE DAY

A large number of attendants could mean a large headache, but for Claire, nine bridesmaids helped turn the day into one long party. They started with a visit to her favorite hair salon for styling and champagne, then had their makeup done. By the time they arrived at the St. Regis to change into their dresses, "it felt like getting ready for a college formal, everyone helping everyone else, drinking champagne, watching British sitcoms on cable. I wasn't even remotely nervous."

Jonathan, on the other hand, was in a bit of a state. After all, he

had a lot on his mind: looking after dozens of friends from overseas, packing for the honeymoon (Claire had had a law exam the day before and had left the packing to him), and trying not to lose the earrings that were his wedding present to his bride. At lunch he watched his groomsmen eat without even looking at the menu himself. Later, "the sheer magnitude of the occasion," combined with a burgeoning case of the flu, nearly did him in. Fortunately, the ushers who were staying with him helped him into his gold-and-red vest.

At a few minutes before five o'clock, as her limousine driver encouraged her to get into her role ("Honey, you've got to make an entrance!"), Claire got out of the car and felt the butterflies start. Walking down the aisle behind the nine bridesmaids and two children, she realized her father was crying. "I was trying to hold it together myself for the sake of the mascara," she claims. Up at the altar, Jonathan's nerves had been replaced by awe. "I had no idea what she'd be wearing, and she looked so angelic, so beautiful. I was amazed to be marrying this woman."

Claire says that she felt as if she were in a dream, until her friend began singing "Ave Maria" and she realized she was actually being married. Holding hands, bride and groom exchanged their vows to love, honor, and cherish, and teared up when they declared devotion "until death us do part." Each time the organist played a British hymn, the right half of the church burst into song, accompanied by the off-key Americans. At the end of the hour-long ceremony, Wiedor's *Toccata* ushered bride, groom, and wedding guests into the December night.

Out on the street, the crowds "parted like the Red Sea" as the twenty-seven-member party walked to the reception. Cars honked, passersby stopped and applauded, flashbulbs popped, and the groomsmen held up traffic. Jonathan says it's probably as close as he'll ever get to feeling like a rock star.

As guests assembled at the St. Regis, the sound of clinking champagne flutes and martini glasses blended with that of a pianist performing holiday carols. Claire, Jonathan, and their families posed for pictures in front of wreaths and a Christmas tree while their guests attacked the caviar.

Upstairs, crystal chandeliers and ivory candles competed with the lights of New York City. Waiters served course after course to a crowd that, Jonathan says, "we mixed up a bit" to keep the conversation lively. In proper British style, the best man gave a fifteen-minute speech that included a reference to Claire's early American ancestors, who he surmised were "rolling in their graves to see her marrying an Englishman."

Following dinner, the couple performed their obligatory first dance to "Moon River"—"After it was over, I knew we were home free," says Claire—then opened the floor to the assembly. The bride and groom cut the cake with a sword; the guests smoked cigars and opened favors—Claire's father, a perfumer, had created a special fragrance called Wedding Day. At midnight the bride and groom departed for their suite, knowing they had an early morning flight. Not so some of their guests, who went club-hopping until sunrise. "We saw some of them at the airport the next day," says Claire. "They looked perfectly miserable."

Summing it up, Jonathan says that aside from marrying the love of his life, the most wonderful part of the day was seeing "all our favorite people in the same room at the same time, sharing our happiness. It was magical."

on christmas weddings:

› SPACES AND SCHEDULES ARE EXTRA CROWDED DURING THE HOLIDAYS, SO RESERVE YOUR CERE-MONY AND RECEPTION SITES EXTRA EARLY, BOOK YOUR PROFESSIONALS FAR IN ADVANCE, AND MAIL YOUR INVITATIONS AT LEAST SIX WEEKS BEFORE THE WEDDING.

› INCORPORATE HOLIDAY TOUCHES—GREENS, CAROLS—BUT AVOID A DICKENSIAN PRODUCTION.

› WITH THEIR LIGHTS, CANDLES, AND TOUCHES OF GOLD AND SILVER, HOLIDAY DECORATIONS ARE MOST BEAUTIFUL AT NIGHT. AN EVENING WEDDING WILL MAKE THE MOST OF THE SEASON.

› *PHOTO TIP:* EVEN WITH ALL THE FESTIVE COLORS, CONSIDER BLACK-AND-WHITE PHOTOGRAPHY; IT WILL GIVE YOUR PICTURES AN OLD-FASHIONED, TIMELESS QUALITY THAT REFLECTS THE SPIRIT OF THE SEASON.

TIPS

summer-inspired weddings

III

HOLLY TURCHETTA AND LING LI **DATE:** SEPTEMBER 9 **LOCATION:** BRIDGEHAMPTON, NEW YORK **CEREMONY:** THE BEACH AT THE BRIDGEHAMPTON TENNIS AND SURF CLUB **MUSIC:** PACHELBEL, CANON IN D MAJOR **READINGS:** KAHLIL GIBRAN, "MAKE NOT A BOND OF LOVE" **RECEPTION:** BRIDGEHAMPTON TENNIS AND SURF CLUB **STYLE:** BAREFOOT FORMAL **TIME:** 5:30 P.M. CEREMONY; 6:00 P.M. RECEPTION **NUMBER OF GUESTS:** 115

For the rare couples who have exceptional vision, a do-it-yourself wedding isn't merely a matter of saving money—it is about using their creative energy to put together a completely original event. This bride and groom met on a photo shoot—she was a magazine beauty editor; he was a photographer assigned to shoot one of her articles—and forged a friendship that eventually turned to romance. A deep appreciation of nature, combined with a gift for exquisite art direction, resulted in a wedding that was charming and elegant, with an element of surprise.

THE PLANNING

"We're watery fish people who like to have the sand between our toes," explains Holly Turchetta, the bride, who had attended scores of country club weddings. Although she and her fiancé, Ling Li, appreciated the rituals held in churches and grand ballrooms, they wanted something essentially loose, casual, and fun, which would reflect the spirit of their relationship. Because they spent much of their time at the beach, their first notion was to have a big free-form barbecue, with their casually dressed guests seated on the dunes or a deck—essentially a nuptial bonfire with maybe a little waiter service. Little by little, as Holly discussed things with her mother—her parents had offered to pay for the event—the wedding became marginally more formal. But the couple's original plan—"We wanted it to be as 'real' as we could make it"—stayed intact, with a seaside location and an atmosphere as relaxed as a day at the beach.

Although they became engaged on February 13 during a Monday evening of television, this self-described "summer couple" knew they wanted to be married when the weather was warm. The weekend after Labor Day seemed ideal. The seasonal rush would have ended, vacationers would have returned home, and the weather would still be fine.

The barefoot bride, looking as comfortable and relaxed in tulle and lace as in a pair of jeans.

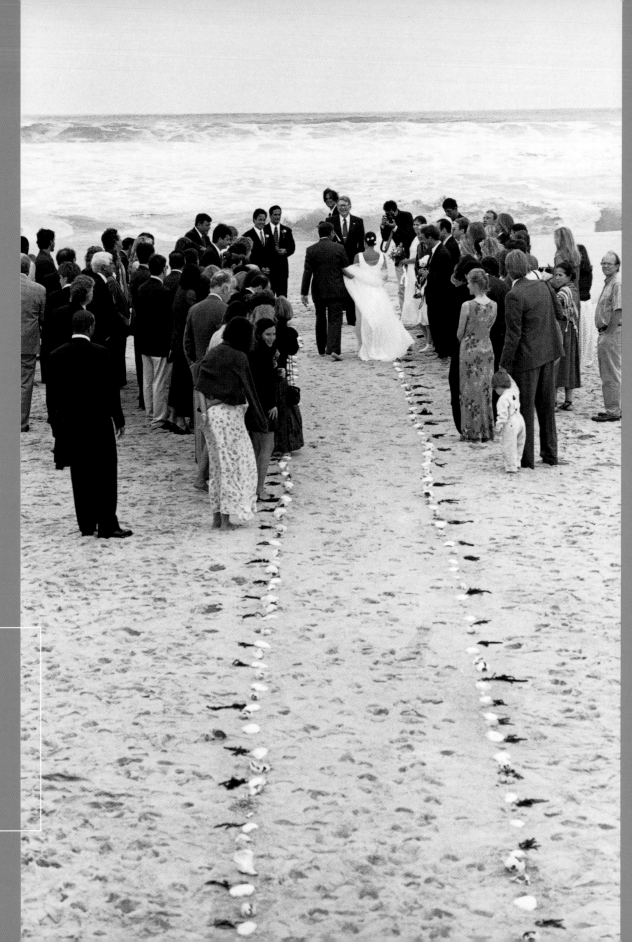

FROM LEFT TO FAR RIGHT: The aisle of shells; a ceremony musician; two generations of guests; Holly and Ling, just after the ceremony; paper lanterns blowing in the wind.

The heart and soul of this production was the beach itself. While discussing logistics with her mother, Holly ruled out a wedding without shelter or even tables, as first envisioned. Next she and Ling went in search of seaside locales in the Long Island town where they spent their summers. They considered renting a house to help keep the party intimate, but then they checked out a beach club on the advice of a friend. It was ideal. A glorified shack masquerading as a private club, it stood right on the sand, and it was run by a congenial woman who told them they could modify it however they liked, as long as it was in good shape when they left. Since the woman planned to close the club for the season in mid-September, the couple could be fairly uninhibited about bringing in their own decorations and lighting. While they loved the outside of the club, the interior was a blank canvas, and Holly and Ling knew that adding personal style would be their biggest challenge.

For the ceremony, only the sand would do. The bride recalls how, until the wedding itself, her family "didn't get it at all." Having raised her as a Catholic, Holly's Rhode Island parents would have liked her to be married in a church ceremony. But she felt uncomfortable with the strict rules, and she became even more concerned when she discovered most Catholic priests will not marry anyone outside of a church. In addition, "Ling would have had to go through the church's marriage preparation thing, which I wasn't too sure about myself." And since Ling hadn't grown up with a religious background, the two went in search of an officiant who would combine the seriousness of their commitment with the casualness of their spirits. The Unitarian minister they eventually located was so sensitive to the bride's family that he even offered to wear a collar.

The beach club rental was strictly bare-bones—no cutlery, no plates, and no linens were included. Holly and Ling rented blue glass plates and stemware, and Holly purchased three hundred frosted glass votive candle holders, also in shades of blue—cobalt, teal, and sea green—for the tables, the bar, and the buffet. She also rented blue-and-white-striped tablecloths and found fish-theme cocktail napkins. And throughout the summer, Holly and Ling collected seashells and beach glass to sprinkle on the tables.

But the one element that made the strongest impact was the lighting; as a photographer, Ling was particularly aware of the mood that lights could establish, and he knew from the start that the bright overhead lights in the club's dining room would have to go. On a trip to New York City's Chinatown he found rice-paper lanterns, which were festive and struck a subtle Asian note. The couple bought lightbulbs in every available color—red, green, orange—to place inside the lanterns. Ling's brother, Sebastian, collected cast-off bamboo stalks from the sides of local roads, and Holly spent weeks scraping and smoothing them for use as lamp supports. Finally, friends helped the couple hang the lanterns from the bamboo poles all over the deck, the beach, and the dining room.

In addition to knowing where to find a lot of bamboo, Sebastian is a wizard with flowers (and with food—he prepared the rehearsal dinner). Holly was thrilled when he offered to do all the flowers as a wedding present, not realizing quite how big a project Sebastian had in mind—he grew the entire wedding from seed. "Gardeny and wildflowery" was how everyone foresaw the arrangements, utilizing seasonal blossoms, including a truckload of sunflowers, cosmos, dahlias, and bachelor's buttons. Instead of standard florist vases, Sebastian borrowed containers from family and friends and let the various shapes and sizes help dictate the final look. Holly and her sister, her only attendant, would carry simple hand-tied bouquets of blue and white, to match the sea.

Planning the food involved much less hands-on participation from the bride and groom. The club had hired a new chef, Brent Newsome, for the summer, which was great news for Holly and Ling; they had heard rave reviews of his cooking from friends who'd eaten at his Hamptons restaurants. The three concocted a menu based on "grilled, beachy summer food" and met several times to refine their ideas.

The music, like the food, seemed to drop into Holly's and Ling's laps. They asked the minister if he knew any classical musicians who would be willing to perform on the beach; he immediately offered the names of two violinists and a viola player he had seen at another seaside wedding. Friends recommended the "Motown-funky-soul" band they had used at their own reception, a group that guaranteed real dance music.

In keeping with their beach theme, the bride created invitations that were in harmony with the sea. For the folded overlay she designed a picture of two intertwined fish and block-printed it on delicate Tibetan paper, using blue ink for one fish, gold for the other. Inside went the semiformally worded invitation card, which was edged in blue. In a bow to traditional etiquette, Holly decided against response cards and instead treasures the handwritten notes of acceptance or regret sent by every invited guest.

As a fashion editor, Holly should have had an easy time finding a wedding dress, but she was almost overwhelmed because she knew too much. After she rejected scores of frilly, princessy dresses, Holly got in touch with Lisa Hammerquist, a New York dressmaker, who encouraged her to "look around, try on stuff, see what you like and what you look good in." Together they collaborated on the dress Holly really wanted—a simple sleeveless gown cut on the bias, with a semi-Empire waist and a lace yoke. The silk underlayer and silk-satin organza top had a sheer quality that worked beautifully with the watery setting. At the last minute the bride and her dressmaker realized the dress needed a dash of romance, so they threw together a tulle stole—Holly ran out and purchased the tulle, Lisa hemmed it up, and the result was a feather-light shawl that draped gracefully in the back.

After the ceremony, the bride, groom, and their families pose for a moment on the beach.

CLOCKWISE FROM FAR LEFT: The groom's uncle; a young guest steps over the line; the kiss; sand removal; spare flowers wait in a bathroom sink; a member of the waitstaff; a guest's essentials, stowed on the stairs.

THE DAY

The gods smiled on Holly and Ling throughout the planning stages of their wedding, but when the day itself dawned, so did near catastrophe. After a monthlong drought, Hurricane Felix hit Long Island. The sea swelled to monstrous proportions; the sky turned gray and threatening; the beach was covered with scum and seaweed. With no alternative indoor location, Holly and Ling crossed their fingers, hoped the rain would hold off, and got to work cleaning up the beach. Then Ling's brother, Sebastian, arrived with a truckful of flowers, and friends began to help with the arrangements. Meanwhile, Ling and another team of friends busily set up the lights, while others formed an aisle from the dunes to the ceremony site using shells that Holly and Ling had collected.

As the ceremony hour approached, the skies seemed to lighten, providing a theatrical cloud structure. Guests arrived and approximated a formal wedding arrangement, with the bride's and groom's contingents on either side of the shell aisle. As Holly walked bare-

foot over the sand on her father's arm, the roar of the surf nearly drowned out the music, and the minister was forced to shout the vows.

Then things took a truly dramatic turn: Holly and Ling watched in shock as a huge wave formed offshore and bore down on the scene. The bride threw her bouquet in the air, grabbed the hem of her dress, and ran for high ground. "Everyone assumed I'd come down with a severe case of cold feet," she said later. The minister, musicians, photographer, and guests dashed, the wave crashed, and the shell aisle was disassembled. Minutes later the mood went from slightly uptight to loose and giggly as everyone gathered in a circle, hugging. "Our families had only met the night before," recalls Holly, "and the wave was a weird, neat thing that brought everyone together."

The paper lanterns were bobbing in the wind on their bamboo poles as the bride and groom walked up to the deck and formed an impromptu two-person receiving line. As the waiters served champagne, the band went into jazz mode. Although tables were assigned, this was an essentially informal evening, featuring a buffet dinner, a first dance—Al Green's "Let's Stay Together"—cake, and plenty of dancing.

"Flaky, casual, and wonderful" is how Holly describes the next few hours of food, dancing, and an "inspired" moment in which her brother and Ling's friends lifted the couple up on chairs, despite the fact that neither was Jewish. "Both of us went into the day itself with a little trepidation, given the fact that our families are so completely different," recalls the bride, "but we ended up being completely in awe of the day—it was so magical." And in a true testament to the fact that even the most unconventional wedding can make everyone happy, Holly watched as her father spent the last few minutes of the reception signing checks, a smile on his face.

TIPS

on beach weddings:

› GUESTS HEAR THE WORD "WEDDING" AND IMMEDIATELY THINK OF DRESSING UP, SO MAKE SURE THEY KNOW THEY'LL BE STANDING IN THE SAND. PROVIDE BASKETS WHERE THEY CAN LEAVE THEIR SHOES.

› STOCK UP ON INSECT REPELLENT AND PLACE IT WHERE GUESTS CAN FIND IT BEFORE HEADING DOWN TO THE SAND.

› A BACKUP LOCATION IS CRUCIAL, EVEN IF IT'S SOMETHING AS SIMPLE AS A COVERED PORCH.

› AN ELABORATE WEDDING GOWN WITH A LONG TRAIN WOULD LOOK OUT OF PLACE IN SUCH A NATURAL SETTING. LOOK FOR A DRESS WITH SIMPLE LINES, KEEP THE VEIL MINIMAL, AND PLAN ON GOING BAREFOOT.

› TELL ALL THE PROFESSIONALS HIRED FOR THE CEREMONY—ESPECIALLY THE OFFICIANT AND THE MUSICIANS—THAT THEY WILL BE PERFORMING ON A BEACH. MUSICAL INSTRUMENTS CAN BE SENSITIVE TO HEAT AND HUMIDITY, AND SOFT MUSIC MAY NOT BE ABLE TO COMPETE WITH THE ROAR OF THE SURF.

› IF YOU PLAN TO SET UP THE DECORATIONS YOURSELF ON YOUR WEDDING DAY, BUDGET AT LEAST AN EXTRA HOUR TO GET YOURSELF READY. WHILE HOLLY'S HAIRDRESSER MANAGED TO WHIP HER INTO SHAPE IN JUST THIRTY MINUTES, IT IS NICE TO KNOW YOU'LL HAVE A LITTLE TIME TO SIT BACK AND JUST BREATHE.

› *PHOTO TIP:* HAVE FAMILY PICTURES TAKEN ON THE SAND. YOU'LL HAVE A BIG OPEN SPACE, A SIMPLE BACKGROUND, AND THE SEASIDE LIGHT, WHICH IS ESPECIALLY FLATTERING AS IT BOUNCES OFF THE SAND. AND PEOPLE TEND TO BE MORE RELAXED ON THE BEACH THAN IN AN INDOOR SETTING.

the professionals

NUMBER OF YEARS IN BUSINESS: Nineteen. He started in his parents' salon when he was eight years old.

WHAT I LOVE ABOUT DOING WEDDINGS: They are a milestone in a person's life, and I like being a part of that. And it usually is a love experience. A lot of my job is to be there and become almost a blanket for the bride, making sure she feels assured that she looks awesome, that her hair is perfect, and that all the details are taken care of. My ultimate goal is to make the bride happy and comfortable with what I'm doing with my part of her day.

HOW I WORK WITH A CLIENT: Some brides are my clients well before they get engaged, but others are referrals whom I may meet for the first time as little as a week before the wedding. I like to communicate as much as possible beforehand and get to know something about the person before I just show up and curl her hair. It helps to see the dress, of course, but I even like to know what kind of guests will be at the wedding, what the families are like. We have a trial day anywhere from a month to a week before the wedding and refine the look. But things always do have a tendency to change on the wedding day itself.

WORKING WITHIN A BUDGET: I charge by the hour, and if I bring an assistant it's more, but what I do during that time varies. Sometimes I can do five people in an hour; sometimes it takes the same amount of time to do just half a person; it depends on the complexity. Generally I work for three hours, styling six to eight people. There are always last-minute requests—to do a grandmother's hair or to give an aunt a blow-out. Not that I mind—that's the nature of the business.

SIGNATURE STYLE: I like natural, beautiful things, so the hairstyles I prefer aren't your normal wedding look—nothing too sprayed and lacquered. I won't push anyone into doing something she doesn't want—hair is a really sensitive issue—but I do like to do something that has a little signature to it, to keep it interesting but gorgeous. Like the Zulu knots I did for Holly. You take good-size locks of hair and just twist and twist and twist, until they curl into little snakes; then you just pin them. Most women wear their hair up for the wedding, because it's a day when they want to do something they don't normally do, something that has a bit more flavor and refinement. But sometimes absolutely straight and simple without even a hint of spray is awesome. What I aim for is not just to make her hair exactly how a bride wants it but to make it look even better.

THE BIG-EAR ISSUE: If someone wants her hair up, but her ears stick out, I do pile some of it up, but I make sure that her ears aren't totally exposed. When it's really a problem, you can always work with hairpieces, flowers, and the veil. There is something so mysterious about veils, in that they partially hide this beautiful style we've created, and then only the husband gets to see the whole thing.

THE MOST COMMON PROBLEM I ENCOUNTER: Women who have just gone too far with their hair. They start doing something like highlights, and then they just do it more and more and more to the point where they have no more natural color at all. At that point it's my job to do less and less and less until we get back to more natural and healthier hair.

MY WEDDING PHILOSOPHY: Weddings are a lot of pressure, but since I have been doing this so long I'm pretty good at handling it. Some hairstylists avoid weddings, but I look at them as a gift, a good thing to be a part of. It's my job, and I make a living doing it, but it's also fun. Hey, it's one big loving party. How can you not have a good time?

FIVE THINGS TO TELL YOUR STYLIST

1. What your dress looks like. Bring a picture!
2. What kind of hairstyles you like. Again, pictures are a big help, or give him an example of a hairstyle you liked in a movie. Even more important, tell him what you *don't* like.
3. The setting of the ceremony and reception.
4. The kind of flowers you're carrying. He might incorporate a few into the hairstyle.
5. What the other people in the wedding party will be wearing, to help give him the overall style of the event.

FIVE THINGS TO ASK YOUR STYLIST

1. His rate and exactly what it covers—how many people, how much time.
2. His spontaneous idea of what he would do with your hair, without any opinion from you.
3. What type of work he likes to do. If it's big and pouffy and you're a wash-and-wear person, you should probably find a different stylist.
4. How much time he's going to need and whether he'll be bringing an assistant.
5. If he will be leaving immediately after doing your hair, find out how you can remove the veil and headpiece at the reception. If one of your bridesmaids can be there during the consultation, he can teach her how to help you.

GILLIAN + PETER

JUNE 28

GILLIAN WYNN AND PETER EARLY DATE: JUNE 28 **LOCATION:** SUN VALLEY, IDAHO **CEREMONY AND RECEPTION:** RIVER GROVE FARM **MUSIC:** THREE SPIRITUALS; STRAUSS-WARSHAUER, "WEDDING SUITE"; BACH, PRAELUDIUM TO CANTATA 29; CARLEBACH, "TOV L'HODOT"; "SIMPLE GIFTS," TRADITIONAL SHAKER HYMN; COUPERIN, "LES BARRICADES MYSTÉRIEUSES"; SPENCE, "AFRINDRAFINDRA"; BACH, CANTATA 208; BREATNACH, "BREATNAIGH ABU"; ISHAM, "A RIVER RUNS THROUGH IT"; VIVALDI, CONCERTO IN D ALLEGRO, PERFORMED BY CHRISTOPHER PARKENING **READINGS:** "SEE THE MOUNTAINS KISS HIGH HEAVEN," SONG OF SOLOMON, THE BLESSINGS FROM THE BOOK OF NUMBERS **STYLE:** FORMAL **TIME:** 6:00 P.M. CEREMONY; 6:30 P.M. RECEPTION **NUMBER OF GUESTS:** 300

The groom grew up fly-fishing in Montana. The bride spent her childhood vacations skiing and horseback riding in the Sawtooth Mountains of Idaho. And although they'd both traveled far from home—Gillian Wynn settling in Santa Monica, Peter Early in London—it was their early love of high peaks, forests, and rivers that suggested a Sun Valley wedding, conceived on a scale as lofty as the mountains themselves.

THE PLANNING

Not only had Gillian known she would get married in Sun Valley "ever since I was born," but it was also the place where the couple met. Despite four years together as Yale undergrads, it was only after graduation, at the Idaho wedding of two fellow classmates, that Gillian and Peter laid eyes on each other. "That first night we ended up smooching in a bar," recalls the bride, to this day baffled by the quirks of fate. After a seven-month long-distance relationship, they decided to abandon California and England and move in together in New York. Six weeks after that, over the Fourth of July weekend, they became engaged in a pizzeria. The next day they flew to Lake Tahoe to announce their plans to Gillian's parents, and her mother asked the question that every newly engaged woman longs to hear: "Honey, what's your fantasy?"

On a brilliant Sun Valley afternoon, Gillian gives her flower girl a hug before heading down the aisle.

When her mom asked what she'd been imagining for her wedding, Gillian didn't skip a beat. *"A Midsummer Night's Dream,"* she replied, laying the groundwork for a production combining awesome natural beauty with a shot of theatrical pizzazz. Focusing on a scene "outdoors in the woods and the trees," Gillian took a fairly minimalist approach to her wedding. Her mother, on the other hand, is a master at staging elaborate events. Together, mother and daughter managed to maintain the essentially natural ingredients Gillian wanted but also to introduce the grand scale and lavish touches a mother of a bride dreams of.

The bride had spent some of her happiest childhood days on the Sun Valley farm of a family friend, Parry Thomas, whom she describes as being like a grandfather. Because his property encompasses a large hunt field—an open parcel of riverside land—it seemed like an ideal place to set up the huge tent that would shelter the three hundred guests, including the couple's friends from childhood, college, and beyond, as well as Gillian's parents' extensive network of friends and business associates from as far away as Australia.

"We wanted to get married sooner," says the bride, but the weather in Idaho tends to dictate the wedding date. Fall would have been a rush; a winter wedding meant coping with weather that might leave guests snowed in—or out. Since June 28 coincided with both her parents' and her grandparents' anniversaries, it seemed a lovely way to keep wedding tradition in the family.

Although Gillian is Jewish, she entered Catholic high school at age fourteen and became a close friend of the principal, Father Richard Rinn, a man whose intellectual approach to religion very much suited her. As the plans proceeded for an essentially traditional Jewish ceremony at which Rabbi Harold Kudan would officiate, Gillian's mother brought Father Rinn into the discussion, knowing that Peter and his family would probably appreciate having their Christian traditions represented.

It's probably impossible for anyone hired to do a wedding as extravagant as Gillian and Peter's not to come at it with all pistons firing. The biggest problem Gillian faced was in getting people to simplify their ideas. "In L.A., I went to see this mock-up tent that the rental people had fixed up to show me, and it looked like Vienna, the sides festooned with all this gauzy stuff. I said, 'Get rid of the swaths, just do a shirred ceiling, and think of the side panels as being as ordinary as a shower curtain.'" Similarly,

she ended up toning down the lighting and making sure she wouldn't be saying her vows under a huppah smothered in hot-house roses. "I wanted to be a bride, not a princess."

A phone call to Polly Schoonmaker, the baker, was the first piece of wedding business Gillian attended to. Seduced by Polly's whimsical cake designs, which she had seen in a magazine, Gillian asked to see photographs of her other work and then spent a week choosing her favorites. For herself she selected a lemon-flavored cake layered with berries, frosted white-on-white, decorated with squiggly "pearls," and topped with a huge sugar rose. For the groom she chose a tiramisu confection on which swam an exqui- site hand-colored school of trout.

Gillian was equally keen about her florist. "As a creative per- son, I know that giving an artist some direction is good," she says, "but that you have just got to have faith in the talent you hire. So I talked to Jennifer about the stuff that was important to me— flowers with a real fragrance, and lots of white—and then said, 'Go!'" Jennifer McGarigle, who flew in from Los Angeles to do the wedding flowers, developed a plan to combine gardenias, peonies, and lilies of the valley in moss-covered pots, clustering

several arrangements in the middle of each table.

For the huppah, Gillian looked to the most creative person she knew, Jane Sterduvan, whose parents, Peggy and Parry Thomas, owned River Grove Farm. Inspired by the botanical invitations, Jane bound birch limbs into four posts, then placed leafy branches between two layers of white organza as a canopy. In the center she hung Jewish prayer shawls, borrowed from close friends and rela- tives of Gillian's family. A god's-eye in the middle, mossy mounds studded with mushrooms at the base of the poles, and a robin's nest with three perfect eggs—the bride's "something blue"—com- pleted the organic and spiritual structure.

Not all of us are lucky enough to count a chef as talented as Wolfgang Puck among our family friends, but Gillian made the most of her connection. In developing a dinner that combined the couple's taste for ethnic foods and indigenous Idaho ingredients, Gillian and Puck came up with a plan that began with two food stations for the cocktail hour. One featured dishes associated with Puck's Spago restaurants—pizzas, potato galettes with smoked trout, lamb satay, and beggar's purses. The other offered Asian morsels like summer rolls and shrimp sukiyaki. To anyone who's

ever been nervous about negotiating with a caterer, Gillian's assertiveness should be an inspiration: when Puck showed her the menu, Gillian actually asked him to change the salad course, requesting Bosc pears and goat cheese instead of his lobster-based dish. The entree was easy: Chilean sea bass, Gillian's favorite dish.

Gillian's personal area of expertise was music—when she met Peter, she was working in digital sound—so she heeded a friend's suggestion and headed directly to a Los Angeles company with access to a huge pool of musicians. Gillian's requests were specific: a brass section, soul singers, and someone who could perform Van Morrison songs. The ten-piece band they assembled

was right on the mark. "These people could practically do anything," enthuses the bride, who even got them to learn the heretofore underappreciated "Stuck in the Middle with You."

They were also expensive—flying ten musicians into Sun Valley and putting them up costs serious money. So when Gillian realized she didn't yet have as much as a flute for the ceremony, she decided to take matters into her own hands and make a CD. Her experience in the music business came in handy for obtaining equipment (she was able to borrow both a studio and state-of-the-art outdoor speakers), and years of listening helped her choose specific pieces, from traditional Russian and Jewish airs to a Celtic

song, "Breatnaigh Abu," which would accompany her grandparents down the aisle. But when it came to the song she would be marching to herself, intuition failed until she talked with her fiancé, who suggested she listen to the theme from *A River Runs Through It.* "When I finally did, I realized it was perfect, especially since Peter was from Livingston, where the movie was filmed."

Carrying on the Sun Valley theme, Gillian ordered invitations made of handmade paper with mountain ferns pressed in it. Formal wording on the parchment overlay gave the specifics; several inserts instructed guests on how to get to Sun Valley, where to stay, and the weekend's party schedule.

"I looked like a cream puff," says Gillian, describing her dress fitting seventeen days before the wedding, during which she realized she couldn't possibly wear the gown she'd ordered. So she hit the streets, drove to an L.A. store that specialized in "unique theatrical dresses that weren't weird," and started going through the racks. A corseted ivory top practically jumped out at her. "It had everything I wanted. The embroidery was taupe, my wedding color, the neckline was this *Emma*–like scoop, which I love, and it even had cap sleeves, for a bit of sweetness." Paired with a straight skirt, it was a little bit Renaissance, a little bit Hollywood, and a lot sexy. And it fit.

THE DAY

Beside a river dwarfed by mountains, three hundred guests opened the wedding program to read words by Lord Byron: "I live not in myself, but I become/Portion of that around me: and to me/High mountains are a feeling." Bach cantatas and spirituals mingled with the wind as the rabbi and priest took their places.

Gillian may be a minimalist, but not when it comes to family and vows. The procession resembled a parade with the Thomases, her honorary grandparents; her grandmother; Peter's grandparents; his parents and their spouses; Gillian's mom on the arms of her two brothers; Peter's brothers; Gillian's sister and her best friend; and the couple's dog, Maddy, who carried the rings in an organza pouch tied to his collar. Then came the flower girl, charming and nervous, followed by Gillian and her dad.

Under the huppah, Father Rinn greeted the guests, admired the setting, and explained his relationship with Gillian, who, he advised Peter, "has a mind of her own." Afterward Rabbi Kudan performed a traditional Jewish ceremony, wrapping the couple in a prayer shawl and giving Peter a glass to smash underfoot. After a hearty "mazel tov" and an even heartier kiss, bride, groom, relatives, and wedding party marched down the aisle to a Vivaldi concerto.

A golf cart took the couple to a nearby friend's house for the *yichud,* the traditional Jewish interlude when the bride and groom privately acknowledge the vows they have just shared. Back at the reception, the guests were devouring the food—even a master entertainer like Puck couldn't have foreseen how deep emotion and mountain air can invigorate three hundred appetites.

The speeches were all extremely personal. Gillian's dad explained why it was so meaningful to have the wedding on his foster father's property; her mother confirmed that seeing her daughter so happy made every bit of the planning worth it; and the groom's two younger brothers toasted Peter and their new sister with affection and humor. Peter read a poem to the bride and talked about the importance of close family ties. Gillian thanked the Thomases and Jane, announced her parents' thirty-fourth anniversary, which was the next day, congratulated two couples who were to be married the next weekend, and then, with a great deal of charm, she beamed, abandoned all eloquence, and gushed that her wedding had been "beyond the fantasy."

Gillian had given the band a long play list, starting with Van Morrison's "Queen of the Slipstream," and including the kind of dance music that gets people to do some serious boogying. Then came the surprise of the evening: Gillian's mom had arranged for a Yale singing group, the Baker's Dozen, to fly in and perform.

The bride's family includes a few traditions at every wedding: a round of Kamikazes ("We're Russian," explains Gillian) and serenading the new family member with a chorus of "Consider Yourself at Home," which Peter received with grace. After nearly five hours of inspired dancing to everything from "I Will Survive" to *Hava Nagila*," the bride and groom stood alone on the dance floor, mugging for the video camera, clearly intoxicated with each other and the magic of the night.

TIPS

on mountain weddings:

› PICK THE WEDDING DATE WISELY. FREAK STORMS CAN HIT AS EARLY AS SEPTEMBER AND AS LATE AS MAY, SO UNLESS YOU SCHEDULE YOUR WEDDING FOR SUMMER, YOU MAY HAVE A SNOWED-OUT CEREMONY. EVEN IN SUMMER, MAKE SURE ALL THE PRINCIPAL PARTICIPANTS ARRIVE AT LEAST A DAY BEFORE THE WEDDING.

› IF YOU HAVE ELDERLY GUESTS OR PEOPLE IN POOR HEALTH, ALTITUDE SICKNESS CAN BE A REAL CONCERN. YOU CAN PLAN TO HAVE A MEDICAL SERVICE STAND BY, OR AT LEAST ARRANGE TO GET SOMEONE TO LOWER GROUND QUICKLY IN CASE OF ILLNESS.

› IF THE RECEPTION WILL BE IN A TENT, MAKE SURE TO RENT ONE WITH HEATERS. MOUNTAIN AIR GETS COLD AT NIGHT, EVEN IN SUMMER.

› SCHEDULE THE CEREMONY FOR THE LIGHT OF DAY, SO PEOPLE CAN SEE WHAT INSPIRED YOUR CHOICE OF SETTING.

› *PHOTO TIP:* IF YOU WANT THE SITE ITSELF EXTENSIVELY DOCUMENTED—THE MOUNTAINS, THE RIVER, AND THE OTHER DETAILS OF THE LANDSCAPE—YOU MIGHT WANT TO BOOK YOUR PHOTOGRAPHER FOR AN ADDITIONAL HALF DAY. THAT WAY SHE'LL FOCUS ON THE PEOPLE DURING THE WEDDING. AND FOR ANY WEDDING WITH MORE THAN TWO HUNDRED GUESTS, IT IS VITAL THAT YOU SET ASIDE AT LEAST TWENTY MINUTES FOR THE PHOTOGRAPHER TO BE WITH JUST THE TWO OF YOU—IT IS ALL TOO EASY FOR YOU TO GET ABSORBED INTO THE CROWD.

florist

JENNIFER MCGARIGLE

the professionals

NUMBER OF YEARS IN BUSINESS: Nine. Three running my own company.

WHAT I LOVE ABOUT DOING WEDDINGS: I have always loved flowers. When I was a little kid and was feeling down, my mom would say, "Why don't you go out and pick flowers?" So weddings are sort of a natural.

HOW I WORK WITH A CLIENT: First I need to know what kind of mood they want to create, what style they like. Do they want it to be formal or casual? Intimate? Rustic? One woman told me she was looking for a dinner party mood, so I went to swap meets and collected a bunch of silver-plated antique containers that would be beautiful vessels for formal arrangements. Knowing the location is also important. I almost always visit it before the event.

Next we discuss colors. Some women want really traditional bridal colors—whites and creams—which you can actually do a lot with. I might suggest we mix it with tangerines and greenery and roots, or that we do arrangements in old collectible pottery, and then add tiny kumquats and geranium leaves, so the orange and green will pop a bit.

Ideally we have two or three meetings. At the first we share basic information, and the client finds out who I am and the kind of work I do. Then I draw up an itemized list, with prices, and I do a sample centerpiece. If someone has asked for something I really don't think will work, I'll give her a sample of that, but I'll always have more ideas to show her. For example, one woman asked for really clean arrange-

ments of a single type of flower per vase—all lilies of the valley, all peonies—but I thought she might like to see what it would look like to mix things up a bit, so I did some samples that combined two or three elements, like green cymbidiums with white lisianthus, and peonies with hydrangeas. When the possibilities are presented to a client, she usually sees that her original idea was perhaps a little limited. It helps a lot when they trust me to do my job.

SIGNATURE STYLE: Sort of moundy, roundy garden flowers and a lot of color blocks. What's really neat about doing a wedding is taking my style and making it suit the individual couple, and ending up with something we all like.

WORKING WITHIN A BUDGET: It is important to know up front if budget is an issue. And don't apologize for it—it is my job to make you feel good and excited. There is always some way of doing something in a unique, peaceful way, no matter how much you have to spend. A smaller budget can mean I get a little more creative, but it always means prioritizing. I ask a client to tell me what's really important to her—the ceremony, the reception, or the personal flowers. It's always better to prioritize rather than spread yourself too thin—that will look cheap. If somebody couldn't afford to have me do everything, I wouldn't hesitate to help them with ideas for the parts of the wedding they could do themselves. For example, I might do the bouquet, the bridal party's flowers, and the ceremony area and then suggest that for the reception they use assorted groupings of candles on the tables, with scattered flower heads and petals at the base. Or they could rent candelabra and trim them with gardenias and miniature oranges.

ONE FAVORITE WEDDING: A woman came to me with a limited budget and a fondness for daisies, which are pretty inexpensive. I thought that was neat, but I didn't want to do anything that looked as if we were obviously saving money. So I made her a nosegay out of butter-yellow English roses, the whole thing collared with daisies and tied with organza. For the bridesmaids, I made really tight clusters of daisy nosegays, and we put daisy bushes all around a gazebo. It looked cool and reflected her taste and wasn't terribly expensive.

THE BIGGEST PROBLEM I ENCOUNTER: People who want things big and showy. Flowers are very intimate; you should let them be what they are.

MY WEDDING PHILOSOPHY: The best part is creating someone's vision. And a great reward comes from working with other people in the wedding who are really good at what they do. I've always loved working with flowers, but doing wedding flowers is probably me at my happiest.

FIVE THINGS TO TELL YOUR FLORIST

1. The basics—date, time, and location of both ceremony and reception.
2. Your budget.
3. The numbers—how many people in the wedding party, how many tables at the reception, special needs like buffet arrangements or tent decorations. Don't forget the entryway—or the ceremony site.
4. The overall style or feel you want, as well as a verbal blueprint of the location—approximate size, any architectural elements or lack thereof, surrounding scenery.
5. The flowers and colors you love. If you think you have no preferences, visit a few floral shops. Your flower memories will come back to you.

FIVE THINGS TO ASK YOUR FLORIST

1. What flowers and materials she prefers to work with. Always ask to see a portfolio of prior weddings and parties.
2. The special touches she envisions for your wedding.
3. Request a sample centerpiece, so you know exactly what to expect.
4. An itemized proposal, down to the last boutonniere.
5. Current letters of reference.

SARAH BUFFEM AND ALEX PRUDHOMME **DATE:** JUNE 24 **LOCATION:** MOUNT DESERT ISLAND,

MAINE **CEREMONY:** THE GROOM'S FAMILY HOME **MUSIC:** BAGPIPERS AND IMPROMPTU GUEST

PERFORMANCES **READINGS:** WALLACE STEVENS, E. E. CUMMINGS **RECEPTION:** JORDAN POND TEA

HOUSE, ACADIA NATIONAL PARK, MAINE **STYLE:** INFORMAL **TIME:** 4:30 P.M. CEREMONY; 6:30 P.M.

RECEPTION **NUMBER OF GUESTS:** 130

Alex Prudhomme's grandparents had built their house by hand in the 1950s on a pocket of coastal Maine looking out on Swans Island. It had been the family's gathering place ever since, where cousins, aunts, and uncles assembled each Labor Day, and it was there that Alex proposed to Sarah Buffem one June evening. As she stood on the rocks wearing a mosquito-proof head net, he got down on one knee and offered her a ring he'd fashioned from dandelions, daisies, and a dried-out lobster antenna. After Sarah stopped crying, they began discussing their wedding.

THE PLANNING

Their hearts embraced the idea of an outdoor Maine wedding, even while their minds were enumerating "the million reasons not to." On the pro side: sentiment and an easy way, they supposed, to keep the numbers down. The cons: the likelihood of cool weather (the house is rented out for most of the summer, so a June wedding it had to be), bugs (Sarah wasn't wearing that mosquito netting for nothing), and the fact that the bride's family was from Rhode Island and had harbored hopes that she'd marry closer to home turf. Sentiment won out.

It was Alex who planned most of the event. In addition to his deep roots in the area, he's "very enthusiastic about organizing parties and getting people together," says Sarah. As a novelist, his flexible schedule also meant he could take time out of his day to make phone calls while Sarah attended to her job as a photographer's assistant and pursued her own fledgling career in fine art photography.

Using the location as their starting point, Alex and Sarah bombarded each other with ideas. The L-shaped house forms a natural amphitheater, an ideal space for a circular ceremony, which was what their Congregational minister suggested and what Sarah had "somewhere in the back of my mind."

Signs painted by the groom's
mother, on boards salvaged
from the 1950s house, direct
guests to parking.

Her grandfather's Quaker background and a wedding Alex had attended the previous winter were further inspiration, as the couple talked about opening the ceremony to guest participation. "Since we weren't doing it in a church, we decided to make it a real celebration," recalls Sarah. Soon they added embellishments: they would each walk out of the woods with their parents, they would marry in the middle of a wedding circle, and their guests would be invited not only to speak but also to bring musical instruments, songs, anything that would add to the spirit of the day. "Our minister did warn us that [the plan] could backfire," but the couple agreed not to worry about awkward silences and unrehearsed speeches.

Besides, they were too busy. Some of the most charming parts of their day were produced by the couple and their families: the invitations (Sarah), the flowers (a friend), and the cake (Alex's sister). Alex was busy hunting down a tent for a backup ceremony location as well as a "true indoor structure for the reception." These two weren't taking any risks as far as the weather went. Alex found the reception location thirty minutes away, in Acadia National Park, where rustic teahouses had been welcoming vacationers since the 1890s. Alex had spent many childhood summer hours eating popovers in the most famous of them, the Jordan Pond Tea House, which he proposed as a perfect party site.

Despite their desire to keep the wedding as intimate as possible, Alex and Sarah were soon in possession of 130 acceptances—with a reception space for only 100. Discussions with the teahouse manager became a bit "animated," according to the bride. "Basically, he just wanted to make sure that the staff would be equipped to handle that size party so early in the season," reports Sarah. After some negotiation, the couple convinced the manager that they could accept service that had a few glitches. In addition to accommodating the couple's special requests for everything from a local blueberry microbrew to letting Alex's sister provide the cake, the staff put together an American repast that included their famous popovers, salmon, and chicken. Says Sarah, "They totally exceeded our expectations."

Both Alex and Sarah felt the woods and water were decoration enough for the ceremony site, and Julia Scott, a family friend renowned for her garden and her wedding flowers, stepped in to add just the right informal note. She ordered potted pansies from a local greenhouse, gathered peonies and daisies from her garden, and collected bucketfuls of local lupines from the Maine countryside. She then tucked them into ceramic jugs and cast-iron pots and placed them on the deck and wooden stairs of the family home.

The ceremony music was easy to choose, if unusual. Alex located two bagpipers, and the couple asked various friends and relatives to bring their own instruments. Scouting for a reception band was somewhat more traumatic. Finally, acting on the advice of the teahouse manager, the couple drove six hours to Portland to listen to a group called the Boneheads. "We were both suffering from mild cases of food poisoning, and when we first heard them we thought they were way too mellow," remembers Alex. But then they kicked things up with a mix of rock and roll, folk, and a

bit of the blues. "We didn't even tell them what to play for our first dance," says Sarah. "We knew they'd do something fun. It was a happy surprise."

The bride made the invitations herself, using an old photographic process called cyanotype, in which objects are placed on a piece of paper that's been hand coated with special chemicals and then exposed to sunlight. The objects she used were maidenhair and Himalayan ferns, the paper was a heavy stock from Italy, the type was simple letterpress, and the wording was traditional. Since both sets of parents were contributing financially, all four were mentioned as hosts on the invitations.

You'd have thought that this homemade wedding would include a dress lovingly sewn by some sentimental relative. Hardly. With its clean lines, body-hugging spandex underskirt, and layers of gossamer and silk-chiffon, Sarah's ankle-length Morgane Le Fay dress was a striking contrast to the rugged Maine coast and a true reflection of her own taste. She went with Alex to pick out his navy Hugo Boss suit, the first one he tried on.

THE DAY

The weather was unseasonably warm and sunny, and three massive bug sprayings kept the insects at bay as guests followed signs that Alex's mother had hand-lettered on old wooden boards salvaged from the original house. Vans transported the group from the parking area down the long gravel drive to the front yard, where they took their seats. Then, led by a bagpiper and flanked by his parents, Alex walked out of one area of the woods while Sarah, with her own bagpipe and parental escort, appeared from another grove of trees, a flower girl leading the way. As they entered the wedding circle, the ceremony began.

Couples often say that the ceremony was too short to remember, but for Sarah and Alex, it was the most exciting part of their day. Within the wedding circle stood the "unofficial-official" party, composed of Sarah's two brothers, her niece, and Alex's two sisters, all of whom entered the circle just before the couple. Everyone stood in silence for a moment, listening to the sea.

One by one, guests came forward and shared their thoughts about the couple, the sense of place, and the "incredible community of people who had come together," as one friend put it. Sarah's uncle played a short piece on his harmonica. Alex's second cousins, who had toured with Pete Seeger, chimed in with "Wild Mountain Thyme." And a friend who'd brought an African drum performed his own tribute.

Finally, the couple stepped into the very center of the circle, their backs to the ocean, to repeat their vows. The minister, Roger Paine, shared their spiritual philosophy: big on family and nature, not so big on organized religion, so the vows were a bit unusual. "We changed some of the wording, but not the meaning," explains Sarah. Alex admits to a bit of last-minute ad-libbing, just to make sure people would listen.

The most dramatic part of the proceedings occurred at the end. Instead of a moment of silence, guests were asked to provide a "moment of noise." They tossed rose petals as an old horn, a tambourine, the African drum, and a quartet of kazoos created a cacophony of sound, climaxing with the pop of champagne corks.

Alex's cousins had decorated "the Tank"—the family's twenty-five-year-old Buick station wagon—with lobster buoys and seaweed, and they used it to chauffeur the wedding couple into Acadia National Park. At the teahouse everyone gathered for cocktails on the deck and drank in the view of Jordan Pond and the Bubbles, a series of mountains that are one of the park's most distinctive features.

CLOCKWISE FROM ABOVE: A cheerful groom; Sarah's upsweep reflects the natural simplicity of the setting; The Tank, decorated with lobster buoys and seaweed; a bucket of Maine essentials.

As Sarah experienced the party, "waiters passed hors d'oeuvres we never tasted, we made the rounds and tried to talk with everyone. Then, at around eight, someone decided we'd better sit down to dinner." The personal testimonials continued as Alex and Sarah toasted each other, a family friend performed a Spanish love song, and a former Yale Whiffenpoof serenaded the bride with "Oh, My Sarah." Even the cake-cutting was extremely personal: Alex's sister, who always baked a pineapple upside-down cake for his birthday, provided the groom's cake, while Sarah had a "heavy-duty chocolate" cake with raspberry filling. Bride fed groom, groom fed bride, and the band played until 2:30 A.M., when the last guests left, clutching homemade packets of lupine seeds. "People still come up to us and say they've never been to a wedding like it." No surprise.

on woodland weddings:

(TIPS)

› SPRAY, SPRAY, SPRAY. WOODS ARE WONDERFULLY ROMANTIC SETTINGS, BUT INSECTS LIKE THEM AS MUCH AS HUMANS DO. IF YOU MARRY IN MOSQUITO SEASON, PLAN THE CEREMONY FOR THE LEAST BUGGY PART OF THE DAY, AND CONTACT A LOCAL INSECT-CONTROL COMPANY.

› THOUGH FORESTS ARE SCENIC, PEOPLE TEND TO FEEL MORE COMFORTABLE IN AN OPEN, SUNLIT SETTING. USE THE WOODS AS A BACKDROP AND HOLD THE CEREMONY IN A WELL-LIT CLEARING.

› NATURE IS ITS OWN DECORATING COMMITTEE. GUSSIED-UP TRELLISES AND ELABORATE FLOWER ARRANGEMENTS LOOK OUT OF PLACE AGAINST A STUNNING NATURAL CANVAS.

› ALWAYS HAVE A BACKUP LOCATION. A TENT, A PORCH, OR A LIVING ROOM CAN BE PRESSED INTO SERVICE SHOULD THE GODS DECIDE TO THROW A DAMP WRENCH INTO YOUR PLANS.

› AN ISOLATED LOCATION REQUIRES FORETHOUGHT REGARDING PARKING. IF A LARGE NUMBER OF CARS WILL DETRACT FROM THE ROMANTIC MOOD, ARRANGE FOR OFF-SITE PARKING.

› "APPROPRIATE" DRESS DOESN'T MEAN YOU HAVE TO OUTFIT YOURSELF LIKE MAID MARIAN. IN A SETTING LIKE THIS, A TRAIN AND VEIL WOULD LOOK TOO STIFF, AND A TULLE SKIRT MIGHT SEEM A LITTLE TOO MUCH LIKE A COSTUME, BUT A LONG, CONTEMPORARY WEDDING GOWN IS PERFECTLY IN PLACE.

› *PHOTO TIP:* A DARK GREEN CEREMONY BACKGROUND TENDS TO PHOTOGRAPH AS BROWN, AND CAN BE UNFLATTERING. IN A SETTING LIKE THIS, BLACK-AND-WHITE FILM CAN ACTUALLY BE MORE BEAUTIFUL THAN COLOR.

lobster bibs for 170

TAMMI VIPPERMAN AND PAUL MCCARTHY **DATE:** AUGUST 19 **LOCATION:** MARBLEHEAD, MASSACHUSETTS **CEREMONY:** THE MARBLEHEAD LIGHTHOUSE **MUSIC:** WAGNER, "WEDDING MARCH" **READINGS:** EXTEMPORANEOUS THOUGHTS FROM A CLOSE FRIEND **RECEPTION:** THE CORINTHIAN YACHT CLUB, MARBLEHEAD **STYLE:** SEMIFORMAL **TIME:** 5:00 P.M. CEREMONY; 5:30 P.M. RECEPTION **NUMBER OF GUESTS:** 170

Tammi and Paul met as teenagers and spent their summer evenings down by the lighthouse, doing what teenagers do. So when they finally became engaged, twelve years later, they didn't have to discuss their wedding location—or even the menu. The lobster boil they held for 170 of their nearest and dearest was a delicious taste of their New England lifestyle.

THE PLANNING

Growing up in seaside New England means that childhood has a nautical motif. In fact, the idea of a wedding anyplace but the local yacht club never occurred to Tammi Vipperman or Paul McCarthy. The bride and groom were extremely close to each other's families: Paul showed the engagement ring to Tammi's father over a game of pool, and on the morning of their engagement, the couple ran to Tammi's house and jumped in bed with her mom. This closeness made the period of wedding planning feel like an eight-month-long group hug. Almost everyone hired to work on the wedding had a personal connection with their families—the florist, the band, even the hairstylist. The few concessions the bride and groom made during the process were because of family. "We picked the things that are *really* important to us and didn't worry too much about other stuff," recalls Tammi. "Our families had been waiting a long time for this, too."

The ideal conditions for Tammi and Paul's wedding featured a "bloodred sunset" and the anniversary of their first date, August 22. What the couple hadn't counted on was boat race week, a time when everything in the Marblehead area is booked solid, including the yacht club and all of the hotel rooms. But this easygoing couple was happy to compromise by choosing an earlier date.

Because they knew the basic reception theme from the start, Tammi and Paul had only a couple of

After fourteen years of dating, a clearly delighted husband and wife.

elements to plan: the outdoor ceremony and the lobster dinner, with enormous emphasis on keeping things casual and fun. They did, however, have to agree on an officiant. Tammi was raised a Baptist, Paul was a Catholic, and the grandparents on both sides were very religious, meaning that a mixed ceremony would please no one. Being married by a justice of the peace seemed too impersonal. As she mulled things over, the bride began thinking about a songwriter, Crawford Bigwell, who was an articulate speaker and one of the couple's closest friends. Wondering if it would be possible for Crawford to marry them, they began a letter-writing campaign to Massachusetts state officials. They received permission in the form of a fax from the governor.

Paul's family background contributed to the ceremony: the couple hired a bagpiper to play traditional Irish music. The bagpipes were also a practical choice, since the sound of waves at a seaside wedding can drown out softer instruments. Tammi, whose heritage is Austrian, considered incorporating her own traditions, but she realized it wouldn't make a lot of sense aesthetically. "I didn't want some guy in lederhosen," she said.

Despite the nautical wedding site, Tammi didn't envision the bridal party in sailor suits; instead, she chose navy blue georgette, which a seamstress fashioned into three differently styled dresses to suit the three physically very different bridesmaids. The men looked no further than their own closets for blue blazers and khaki pants; Tammi shopped at Brooks Brothers for the ushers' blue-striped rep ties and Paul's red four-in-hand. The attendants' accessories were presents from the bride and groom: antique pocket watches for the men, earrings made of local blue stones for the women.

As easy as most of the planning was, the bride and groom still faced the vexing guest-list dilemma. In this case, as in most, the problem arose from numbers. Tammi's original list included fifty people; Paul's mom wanted to invite 190 guests, including some cousins and friends whom the couple had never met. ("Paul's family makes friends easily," explains Tammi.) After discussing the problem with Tammi, Paul had a "tough but honest" talk with his mother, and the paring process began.

Tammi's approach to the element that causes some women the most trouble—the flowers—was direct and simple. Sitting down with a Marblehead florist for a half hour two weeks before the wedding, she described her ideas for the bouquets. For her own, she wanted big garden roses, asters, bluebells, and purple daisies, all of which grew locally. For the bridesmaids, she thought yellow and white roses would look crisp against their navy dresses. Gardenias would suit the mothers and grandmothers, and the men would wear rose boutonnieres.

Her one obsessive goal, oddly enough, was buckets. Tammi wanted the fabric aisle runner that would lead to the lighthouse to be anchored with old-fashioned blue-and-white enamel buckets full of wildflowers. She turned several hardware stores inside out searching for them, but they were nowhere to be found. She finally purchased thirty-two galvanized buckets, which Paul's father spray-painted white. After the ceremony, they were transported to the country club and used as centerpieces.

Deciding who would cater the dinner was a no-brainer, since the Corinthian Yacht Club held a lobster boil every Sunday evening in summer and had hosted over a hundred weddings. The bride and groom had tucked into the club's Sunday dinner on scores of occasions, and decided to stick strictly to tradition, only adding more hors d'oeuvres than usual (coconut-dipped shrimp, stuffed mushrooms).

Although they had been together for a dozen years, the couple still had conflicting ideas regarding reception music: she wanted a DJ playing 1980s hits; he wanted a band with a Motown sound. Polling their families, they went with a majority vote and shopped around for a band. Providentially, Tammi's father had a tenant, Sandy Martin, in nearby Salem, who sang with a band and whom almost everyone in both families had heard at some point. Paul took responsibility for talking with Sandy about specific songs and sought Tammi's counsel about singing a couple of special numbers onstage with her dad and his friends.

Tammi and Paul, who share a strong visual sense, agreed to keep their invitations lighthearted and graphic: clip art featuring

MS 6044

two rings joined together. "Simple but cute" is how Tammi describes the 1950s-style design. Combined with traditional wording, it sent a message that this wedding would combine a respect for ritual with some good-natured humor.

Trusting her mother's tears, Tammi initially ordered a dress as big as a ball gown, with a huge skirt and plenty of ruffles. "It was so beautiful when I tried it on, with all this fabric dragging on the ground," recalls the size-two bride. But the necessary alterations seemed to take the romance out of the dress. "When I got it hemmed and fitted, I felt like a piece of candy." A month later, in a chance visit to a consignment shop, Tammi found a Priscilla of Boston dress from 1968 that was almost identical to the one her mother had been married in, with a mantlelike train attached to the shoulders. After buying it, she spent weeks worrying about how to tell her mother, and instead took her grandmother into her confidence during a bridal shower. Her grandmother's words of assurance—"It's so beautiful, you have to wear it"—encouraged Tammi to go ahead and tell her mom everything. Her reaction couldn't have sounded sweeter to a daughter's ears. "My mom took one look at it and said, 'It's *my* dress!'" recalls a clearly relieved Tammi.

FROM LEFT TO FAR RIGHT: Tammi and her father proceed toward the aisle; a bagpiper leads Paul and the groomsmen to the lighthouse; bride and groom make a triumphant exit.

THE DAY

On the morning of the wedding, the stylist arrived with a batch of "secret hair," to fill in the bride's upsweep, and ornamented it with two tiny enamel flowers. Afterward the bride and her attendants drove to the club for mimosas and makeup.

Meanwhile the father of the bride, while trying to pick up the wedding cake, sat in a traffic jam. The cake got a little "soft and funky" on the drive to the club, so an artistically inclined friend of the bride covered it with flowers plucked from a field.

Just before five o'clock, Paul and his groomsmen followed a bagpiper to the ceremony site as Tammi and her dad stepped out of his 1968 Camaro, headed for the lighthouse, and both started crying. "I was walking down the aisle, trying to keep my makeup from running, kicking over all the buckets full of flowers," Tammi recalls. At the base of the lighthouse a small swarm of children sat clutching tulle bags of birdseed. As Crawford, the officiant, began the ceremony, Paul became so emotional that "he was practically in convulsions." Tammi was still crying, too. "I said 'I do' in the middle of nowhere," she admits. Then the bagpiper piped, the guests threw birdseed, and everyone proceeded to the yacht club, where a phalanx of boys and girls from the Corinthian swim team

CLOCKWISE FROM BELOW: Aisle-rimming buckets now used as centerpieces; the Corinthian Yacht Club; a guest attacks his dinner; the honor guard with paddle boards; tools of the feast; a last dance at the evening's end.

created an arch with their blue paddleboards.

After the hour-long cocktail party, things proceeded apace: the crowd sat for bowls of New England clam chowder, then lined up for the buffet, tied on lobster bibs (they were piled on tables along with lobster crackers and moist towelettes), and tucked in. Though Tammi knew what their first dance would be (Patsy Cline's rendition of "Crazy"), she wasn't prepared for Paul and his friends to climb onstage and serenade her with "Brown-Eyed Girl." She started weeping all over again, as did her mom when her dad sang "You're Still the One."

Another emotion compelled the bride to smash a piece of the cake into Paul's face. Fortunately for her makeup, he responded well and gently fed her a tiny piece of "the best wedding cake I've ever had." Summing it all up, Tammi says, "Until that day the last-minute details had been so intense, we would have told anyone else to elope. But it was just the greatest day."

TIPS

on yacht club weddings:

› ONCE YOU HAVE CHOSEN A NAUTICAL SETTING, REALLY USE IT. PLAN TO HOLD THE CEREMONY AS CLOSE TO THE WATER AS POSSIBLE, BUT BE SURE YOU HAVE A BACKUP LOCATION IN CASE OF RAIN.

› LET THE KITCHEN DO WHAT IT DOES BEST. IF A CLUB IS KNOWN FOR ITS SUNDAY LOBSTER BOIL— OR EVEN A PANCAKE BRUNCH—RECOGNIZE THAT IT IS PROBABLY THEIR MOST SUCCESSFUL MEAL. DON'T ASK A YACHT CLUB TO TURN OUT HAUTE CUISINE.

› TAKE CARE NOT TO GO OVERBOARD WITH A NAUTICAL MOTIF. APPRECIATION FOR THE SITE IS ONE THING; USING THE THEME FROM *THE LOVE BOAT* FOR YOUR FIRST DANCE IS ANOTHER.

› IF YOU ARE MARRYING IN ANY PUBLIC SPACE, LIKE A LIGHTHOUSE, BE PREPARED FOR UNINVITED GUESTS. PEOPLE LOVE WEDDINGS, AND YOU ARE LIKELY TO DRAW A CROWD.

› MOTORIZED BOATS CAN MAKE YACHT CLUBS NOISY PLACES. LET THE OFFICIANT KNOW IN ADVANCE THAT HE WILL HAVE TO SPEAK UP.

› *PHOTO TIP:* A MARINA SOUNDS LIKE A GOOD BACKDROP FOR PICTURES, BUT BE WARNED THAT BOBBING MASTS AND FLAPPING SIGNAL FLAGS CAN CROP UP IN ALL THE WRONG PLACES. YOU DON'T WANT YOUR MOTHER LOOKING AS IF A SAILBOAT MAST IS GROWING OUT OF HER HEAD. IF YOUR PHOTOGRAPHER SUGGESTS USING A LESS BUSY BACKDROP, SHE PROBABLY HAS A GOOD REASON.

fantasy-inspired weddings

IV

13

CHRISSE + JOE

(JUNE 14)

CHRISSE OTIS AND JOE NORTON DATE: JUNE 14 LOCATION: GLEN ELLEN, CALIFORNIA CEREMONY AND RECEPTION: BELTANE RANCH MUSIC: PACHELBEL, CANON IN D MAJOR; SELECTIONS FROM MOZART AND VIVALDI READINGS: SANSKRIT PROVERBS AND PERSONAL VOWS STYLE: COUNTRY FORMAL TIME: 4:00 P.M. CEREMONY; 4:45 P.M. RECEPTION NUMBER OF GUESTS: 180

Although they both attended the University of California at Santa Barbara and had hundreds of mutual acquaintances—the bride says they have "about one degree of separation"—this San Francisco couple didn't meet until they attended the New Orleans Jazz Festival. It was there that they fell in love over fried food and hurricane drinks outside the gospel tent. Four years later, when they became engaged, it was obvious that their wedding would take its cues from both locations, with a zydeco band and great food and drink served up on a northern California ranch.

THE PLANNING

An hour after Joe Norton popped the question on a vacation in Hawaii, he and Chrisse Otis were drinking champagne and talking on the phone with their parents. "Joe's mother loves to organize things—we're very similar that way—and we pretty much started planning things that day," Chrisse says. Luckily, the bride and her fiancé's mom also shared the same idea of where to have the wedding: somewhere in the Sonoma Valley, where the couple had one of their first dates—"Way crazy fun" is how Chrisse remembers it. The loose, outdoorsy, rambling style they came up with was a mix of many influences.

They realized how comfortable and loving a wedding could be long before they began planning their own—two years before, in fact, at a friend's East Coast ceremony. "It was the most amazing wedding we had ever been to, so much about the couple," says Chrisse. Setting their sights on the same kind of elegant but informal ambience, they hired Mary Ellen Murphy, a San Francisco–based wedding coordinator, and headed into wine country to scout locations.

It almost never rains in northern California in summer, so the wedding would definitely be out-doors. Looking for something less commercial and more low-key than a functioning winery, they vis-ited every potential venue from mansions to a grotto, but they knew "the second we saw it" that

Chrisse's brilliant bouquet explodes against her snow-white dress.

they would be tying the knot at Beltane Ranch. The egg-yolk-yellow five-bedroom bed-and-breakfast with wraparound porches looked as if it had been transported from Louisiana. In fact, Beltane—now a working olive oil farm—was originally a brothel, founded by a New Orleans madam who had moved west. Surrounding the structure were huge vats of wildflowers, big antique milk pails, balls of barbed-wire fencing, an old yellow truck that matched the house, and fields where cows and horses grazed. Chrisse and Joe were so taken with the place that they allowed the location to dictate their wedding date. "Beltane books up really quickly, so we had to be flexible," recalls Chrisse. They

took the only date available for the following summer, giving themselves ten months for preparations.

"Amazing" is a word Chrisse sprinkles throughout her conversations about the wedding, and she means it—especially when she's describing Mary Ellen Murphy, who helped the couple find Beltane. She also scanned directories of caterers, bands, and florists and presented Chrisse with a list of her top five candidates in each category. "She ended up being one of our closest friends," says the bride.

The only pro the bride found herself was florist Kate Stanley, whose arrangements Chrisse and Joe had admired at a Napa wed-

ding. "I hadn't given two thoughts to the flowers," declares Chrisse, "until I went to my friend's wedding and completely focused on them." She met with Kate and talked about coordinating the colors with Beltane's lavender-and-yellow color scheme. To contrast with a pure white wedding dress, they sketched a bridal bouquet of magenta, purple, and deep apricot flowers tied with chartreuse ribbon; white blooms for the bridesmaids; and for the junior bridesmaids, garlands of miniature blossoms as well as moss-lined wire baskets. For tossing, they chose thousands of white rose petals nestled inside simple paper cones. They decided to plant lavender and yellow flowers in antique silver teapots for

centerpieces; the head table would feature a checkerboard of tiles and moss interspersed with small floral arrangements. Joe's one stipulation was that there had to be sunflowers, which, along with purple hydrangeas, Kate stuffed into old sap buckets and fastened onto oak trees. One of her most beautiful touches was the lighting: strings of white lights and Japanese lanterns along the top story of the bed-and-breakfast, which were lit as the sun went down.

Although Mary Ellen gave Chrisse a list of caterers in several price categories, the bride hired Elaine Bell, the premier caterer in wine country, without a second thought. "She's definitely on the expensive side, but food was our biggest priority," explains the

bride. Relying almost exclusively on local ingredients, Elaine organized a tasting for Joe and Chrisse and then fine-tuned the menu.

Partly in memory of their first meeting, and partly because it is just good dancing music, Chrisse and Joe wanted a Cajun zydeco band. Mary Ellen let them know that a local group called the Swamp Dogs was playing an earlier wedding, also at Beltane, so the bride and her mother "kind of snuck in" and gave a thumbs-up to the seven-piece band, which featured a woman on washboard and spoons, along with guitars, a drum, and a fiddle. For the ceremony, Mary Ellen suggested the Lawrence String Quartet. They sent Chrisse a tape and a list of possibilities, including Mozart and Vivaldi, which her father helped her edit into a harmonious medley.

Chrisse found her dress at a London designer's trunk show that was sponsored by Alençon, a local boutique. Made of dozens of yards of white silk taffeta, it featured a Fortuny-style pleated bodice, a drop waist, a long side-slit skirt, and a huge bustle.

The dress was breathtaking, but it was a nightmare to produce; every time the material came from the mill, it had a black line running through it. The dress was supposed to have been delivered in March, but May came and Chrisse's first fitting had to be canceled for the third time. "I lost my mind at three o'clock that morning, when I sat up in bed, called the boutique, and screamed into their voice mail, 'I'm fighting with my fiancé, my head is spinning

around, and I've been dreaming about this dress since I was three years old!'" recalls the bride, who admits that she's still horrified by her reaction. But apparently hysteria does work on occasion, and the dress arrived shortly thereafter.

In fact, Chrisse says that Alençon's owner was "a professional and a doll" throughout the torturous episode. Completing her ensemble were a long veil with a short blusher veil attached to a headband of pale green flowers, and a pair of white sandals trimmed with daisies.

Ordering the bridesmaids' dresses was nearly as traumatic: three arrived in the wrong size, having been shipped by a company that immediately went out of business. Chrisse counts herself lucky that the shop's owner from whom she'd ordered the gowns was persistent enough to locate the original designer and persuade him to alter the dresses—ice-blue skirts with shiny satin Empire waists and double georgette skirts.

To announce the event to family and friends, the traditionally worded invitations were printed in periwinkle blue on white paper. What made them just a little different was the response cards. Instead of asking guests to check off "accepts" or "regrets," Chrisse ordered cards that simply requested a response by May 25. The handwritten replies were as varied as the guest list itself, ranging from drawings and verses to the kind of impeccably worded note that Emily Post would have applauded.

CLOCKWISE FROM FAR LEFT: A token of affection; an antique teapot filled with flowers; Chrisse gets a hand with her yards of silk taffeta; the head table, with its checkerboard centerpiece; after months of torture, the dream dress; the working side of Beltane Ranch.

After the ceremony, the newly-weds stroll into the sunlight.

THE DAY

It was probably good that Chrisse and Joe respected tradition and spent the night before the wedding apart. After returning to her hotel from the rehearsal dinner, the bride spent an hour dancing around buck naked in her veil before realizing she should get some sleep. The next morning she met up with her new friend, wedding coordinator Mary Ellen, for a morning run. Afterward the makeup artist arrived, and the bride and bridesmaids sat down for a long session with concealer and lipstick.

Meanwhile, the men of the wedding party played basketball before suiting up. The five groomsmen and two additional ushers wore blue blazers, stone-colored dress pants, azure shirts, and gold ties. Joe dressed up his navy blue suit with a gold tie. ("He's as much of a clotheshorse as I am," notes Chrisse.) The men left for pictures at the ranch, followed by the women of the wedding, Chrisse and her endless lengths of silk taffeta being pushed, pulled, and prodded into the car by two bridesmaids.

At Beltane, guests arranged themselves in chairs under the oak trees and along the shady porches. Joe and the groomsmen stood beside a fountain in the gravel courtyard, where the backdrop included two nonfunctioning outhouses painted in the ranch's signature pale yellow. Chrisse and her attendants waited on the second-floor porch and descended one by one to the strains of the string quartet. The junior bridesmaids, in Laura Ashley dresses and Mary Janes, were as fresh and charming as the setting, and the bridesmaids looked like cool drinks of water in their blue gowns.

Then entered Chrisse, beyond beautiful and utterly composed. When her veil snagged on a tree, she gave it a firm, eloquent yank and continued on her way.

At the base of the stairs she joined her divorced parents, who walked their daughter down the short wedding aisle. The fathers of the bride and the groom contributed the most moving parts of the ceremony: Chrisse's dad recited a Sanskrit proverb, and Joe's father read words he'd written himself about monogamy and love. After the groom stopped crying, Chrisse got her own chance to weep as she and Joe read the vows they'd written together, a process that "brought them so close, all over again." They spoke briefly about the moment they fell in love, about commitment, and about marriage. And they were wed.

Immediately after being proclaimed husband and wife, Chrisse and Joe did the required kissing and hugging, but then retreated upstairs by themselves to one of the bedrooms, where they had some time alone to think "holy cow," to drink champagne, and to sample the hors d'oeuvres. Back at the reception, the Swamp Dogs were laying into it, and everybody was dancing.

As the party swung on and guests carried their plates to the interlocked tables, Chrisse displayed her unique sense of style by lifting her dress's bustle and hauling it over the back of her chair, which made it look rather like a very pretty white mushroom. The pose was short-lived, however, as the band soon struck up the couple's first dance, "Closer to You," which Dennis Quaid had

CLOCKWISE FROM ABOVE: The bridal table; an accordion player, essential to the zydeco sound; Chrisse and Joe's first kiss; four different flavors covered with roses and ivy; Chrisse's dress-as-mushroom.

recorded on the sound track of *The Big Easy*. Although she and Joe "don't really know how to dance," according to Chrisse, it felt great. "I hope it *looked* like dancing."

Despite their guests' good-natured jeering, neither bride nor groom complied with the demands to smoosh cake in each other's faces. Partly it was respect for the four fabulous layers (chocolate royale, gazelle, V.S.O.P., and lemon-frambroise) decorated with lemon-yellow roses and a trail of ivy. Partly it was concern for Chrisse's dress. But at the close of the wedding, pure emotion overcame every thought of preserving her gown. "At the end of the evening I was so happy, I just picked up one of the kids who'd been playing in a mud puddle and gave her a big old hug. I still haven't worked up the courage to get my dress from the dry cleaner."

TIPS

on ranch and farm weddings:

› HOWEVER RUSTIC THE SETTING, A BRIDE IS ENTITLED TO DRESS THE WAY SHE WANTS. CHRISSE ADMITS SHE'D BEEN THINKING ABOUT HER DRESS SINCE SHE WAS A TODDLER. DON'T FEEL THAT YOU HAVE TO WEAR A PRAIRIE-STYLE PERIOD GOWN OR ANYTHING EVEN REMOTELY WESTERN.

› RANCHES COME WITH A VARIETY OF SCENTS—FRAGRANT WILDFLOWERS, SWEET GRASS, AND BARNYARD ANIMALS. HOLD THE CEREMONY AND RECEPTION WHERE THE COWS AND HORSES ARE A FEAST FOR THE EYES RATHER THAN AN OFFENSE TO THE NOSE.

› IF IT RAINS, DIRT WALKWAYS WILL BECOME MUDDY OBSTACLE COURSES. RENT COVERINGS TO PRO-TECT THE PATHS LEADING FROM THE MAIN HOUSE TO A TENT AND OUT TO THE PARKING LOT AS WELL. RECRUIT A COUPLE OF THE GROOMSMEN TO CARRY YOU TO THE AISLE. IN ADDITION TO SAVING YOUR SHOES, YOU'LL BE MAKING QUITE AN ENTRANCE.

› MAKE HAY WHILE THE SUN SHINES. SINCE A BIG PART OF A RANCH'S APPEAL WILL BE THE OUTDOOR SETTING, TIME THE PARTY SO THAT EVERYONE WILL BE ABLE TO SEE THE SURROUNDINGS IN THE CLEAR LIGHT OF DAY.

› *PHOTO TIP:* EVEN IF YOU ARE USING ONLY A SMALL PART OF THE RANCH PROPERTY FOR YOUR WED-DING AND RECEPTION, TAKE ADVANTAGE OF THE OPEN SPACES AND HAVE SOME PICTURES—ESPE-CIALLY OF THE TWO OF YOU—TAKEN AWAY FROM THE PARTY. THEY'LL CAPTURE THE WIDE SKIES AND FIELDS THAT MAKE A RANCH SUCH A BEAUTIFUL WEDDING BACKDROP.

bridal couturiere
NANCY TAYLOR

NUMBER OF YEARS IN BUSINESS: Nine.

WHAT I LOVE ABOUT DOING WEDDINGS: Designing bridal gowns gives me an opportunity to be creative, work with the best possible fabrics, and deal with a unique clientele—generally professional women with great taste.

HOW I WORK WITH A CLIENT: Since my business is by appointment only, our first meeting will be by phone. My staff and the caller will screen each other. One of our salespeople will describe exactly what we offer, which is our line of sample dresses, along with the chance to alter just about any part of any dress, as well as the option to order a one-of-a-kind gown. We describe the fabrics we use—silk, cotton, and linen—and go over our price range.

If everything's a go, our first in-shop meeting takes about an hour, during which a salesperson finds out about the specifics of the wedding—the date, time, and location—and has the bride try on samples. Most women immediately tell us what they like or hate about their bodies. It is usually their bustline—some think it is too big, but most think it is too small; we probably sew pads into half the dresses we make. It's fine to bring in pictures of dresses, but it's definitely not necessary. In fact, I find it frees up the process *not* to have a specific dress

in mind. We bring out silhouettes that the client is interested in, and then we might suggest something we feel may be even more flattering for her figure. About 70 percent of our brides find a dress that is just right; the other 30 percent combine parts of two dresses—maybe a neckline from one along with a detail from another. Occasionally a bride will want something unique, like a custom lace from France or a bias-cut dress that we drape over her body.

We do a total of four fittings, which alleviates the need for alterations. After the first in-shop meeting we create a muslin pattern, to make sure we're all talking the same language. After that we cut the fabric, and then we work with a headpiece and veil. The last meeting is a complete run-through with all the accessories. Four fittings sounds like a lot, but it makes everyone much more comfortable with the process.

MY SIGNATURE LOOK: Ours are period dresses with a modern twist. The influences are largely Victorian, simply because it was such a beautiful and ornate era of dressing, but we don't do costume gowns. There is always a simplification in the cut or a change of fabric that makes our dresses modern. We also draw inspiration from the European couturiers' collections, which helps us stay current but not faddish. And I like a bit of Edwardian detail, for formality's sake.

ON WORKING WITHIN A BUDGET: We sell samples at half price at the end of the season, which is a great way for a woman who wears a size eight to get a bargain.

ONE FAVORITE BRIDAL GOWN: A French net-lace bias-cut sheath with cascades of shells and freshwater pearls descending to a fishtail train. Okay, so maybe only one bride in a million will go for it. But it's different and beautiful—it's art.

FIVE THINGS TO TELL YOUR BRIDAL SALON

1. What you'd like to play up—or down—about your body.
2. The setting for the ceremony and reception, as well as the number of people involved—a church with three hundred people, or a backyard with fifty guests.
3. If the wedding is local or away. If it is away, the salon will need at least two additional weeks for shipping.
4. If the client sees herself as a traditional bride, or if the very idea of shopping for a wedding dress feels strange. You should talk about the style you want—soft and feminine, 1950s cool, or something really period.
5. How much you can spend without breaking the bank.

FIVE THINGS TO ASK YOUR BRIDAL SALON

1. What is the most flattering silhouette for your figure and what is most appropriate for your style of wedding.
2. The cost of the dress and whether or not there's a charge for alterations.
3. What the lead time is—that is, how soon they need you to commit to a specific dress. If you're getting married in peak season—May through October—you'll need to order your gown at least six months in advance.
4. How many fittings you will need.
5. Who will do the sewing and alterations.

the professionals

wedding consultant
MARY ELLEN MURPHY

NUMBER OF YEARS IN BUSINESS: Two. In a "previous life" she was director of catering for the Sonoma Mission Inn.

WHAT I LOVE ABOUT DOING WEDDINGS: Sitting down with a client and coming up with exciting ideas. There aren't many jobs in which you become so close to a family, especially in a position where they really trust you; the fact that it's a wedding elevates your importance in the whole scheme. Unlike people who work for a big corporation, I get to see the total picture; every weekend all the pieces I've been working on come together. It's always different—the families, the entertainment, the way it all looks. I'm never bored.

HOW I WORK WITH A CLIENT: The first time I sit down with a client I try to get a feel for what she's after. I always ask, "When you close your eyes and see your wedding day, what do you see?" Even a bride without a really clear vision will come up with a key word that I can work with. At that point I throw out a million ideas, and if the client doesn't grab one, that's okay—but usually something will click. For a woman who was bored with traditional wedding music, I suggested a gospel choir. Another bride said she wanted to make the party a gift for her guests, and I suggested a caricature artist, who was the hit of the reception.

One woman said she wanted magical music during the cocktail hour, and I came up with a band from the Andes. Someone might want a location that her guests have never seen before. Most women want people to get back in their cars thinking, Wow, what a party!

WORKING WITHIN A BUDGET: As long as you have a realistic idea of what your money is going to buy, I'm happy to work within a budget. For example, if a woman comes to me with $7,000, a guest list of 125, and the idea that she can do something fabulous in wine country, I'll ask in the nicest way possible whether that amount will cover anything besides the food. I don't want to shatter anyone's dreams, but there is generally a minimum they need to be prepared to spend for a big wedding. On the other hand, I'm delighted to do small parties that don't go into five figures. They can actually be the most fun of all.

MOST LAVISH PRODUCTION: A million-dollar summer wedding masquerading as a Moroccan marketplace, with a carpeted tent, whirling dervishes, belly dancers, and Louis Roederer Cristal champagne.

MOST INTIMATE WEDDING: A surprise wedding in the High Sierras. At first I was a little hesitant, since the guy had no idea that a wedding was being planned, but my client said not to worry, since he was always bugging her to get married. So I came up with an idea for a horseback ride at sunset on top of a mountain, with a catered dinner for two. I got permission to use the state park, then had to figure out a place for the bride to stash her dress—we ended up hiding it behind a tree. At a certain point in the ride, she told her boyfriend she had to stop and attend to nature. A few minutes later he rode up to where she'd vanished, and found her in her wedding dress, standing beside the minister while violins were playing. The groom was still crying the next day.

MY WEDDING PHILOSOPHY: A good wedding consultant will listen to a client's fantasies, then help her expand on them. I get excited from what I'm doing when someone comes to me with a few ideas. I have the best job in the world.

FIVE THINGS TO TELL A WEDDING CONSULTANT

1. The budget—without it she cannot proceed.

2. How you see your wedding—the location, the style. Key words like "casual," "country," or "elegant" can really help her formulate ideas.

3. The number of guests. This will give her a starting point, particularly in terms of finding a location.

4. How the couple met and courted and how he proposed. The specific story isn't so important, but it provides a lot of information. Knowing whether he proposed on a mountaintop or in the best restaurant in town will help her figure out your basic personalities.

5. Your cultural and religious backgrounds and family histories. This helps build a framework for the event.

FIVE THINGS TO ASK A WEDDING CONSULTANT

1. What a wedding consultant does.

2. Her fee and what exactly it buys, in terms of time, overall planning, and the details she will handle.

3. How many weddings she does each week. You want individual attention, and you need to find out if you're working with a wedding mill or a personalized service.

4. Her background, how long she has been in business, and how many weddings she has coordinated.

5. The worst disasters she has encountered and how she handled them. There's no better way to establish a relaxed relationship between you and your consultant.

KIMBERLY STAHLMAN AND MICHAEL KEARNS DATE: SEPTEMBER 1 **LOCATION:** HEALDSBURG,

CALIFORNIA **CEREMONY AND RECEPTION:** FIELDSTONE WINERY **MUSIC:** "PENNIES FROM HEAVEN"

READINGS: EXTEMPORANEOUS THOUGHTS FROM THE BRIDAL PARTY **STYLE:** INFORMAL

TIME: 5:30 P.M. CEREMONY FOLLOWED IMMEDIATELY BY THE RECEPTION **NUMBER OF GUESTS:** 70

Originally from California but now living in the eastern United States, both Kimberly Stahlman and Michael Kearns wanted to give their friends a wonderful weekend together and introduce the eastern contingent to the best of the West: northern California's scenery, food, and wine. The result was a magical evening on the rustic picnic grounds of an Alexander Valley vineyard.

KIMBERLY + MICHAEL

SEPT I

THE PLANNING

Michael grew up at the beach, a true nature boy. Kim loves anything with historical resonance. Although they now live outside of New York City, their roots are in the West, where they met well over a decade ago. "We wanted a wedding that would be a celebration of this thing so long and slow in the making." While not rejecting tradition, this couple discovered that it was possible to create a very adult wedding that had more to do with their history than with any predictable pattern. Finding the site was the first piece of the puzzle. California's wine region is known for its mansions and estate-like vineyards, neither of which appealed to them. ("We didn't want to rent someone else's house for a day.") Looking for "a natural canvas without constraints," Kim spent three days scouting the area with Michael's mother. What they found was an old stone working winery with a view of the hills and hollows of the Alexander Valley. Essentially a picnic site with benches, it provided the physical necessities—a kitchen, a parking area, and bathrooms—but it didn't impose any particular style. As far as the date went, they planned for the moon to be full, the day to be temperate, and the grapes to be ripe—in other words, the beginning of September.

Since neither the bride nor the groom predicted terribly strong suggestions from their families, they were free "to introduce humor" and to make the wedding as formal or informal as they wanted, recalls Kim. Neither was particularly religious, and so they decided to have one of Michael's close friends deputized for the day in order to perform the ceremony. With two attendants each and only

The bride's bouquet of
flowering herbs, olive branches,
and roses.

a row of mismatched folding chairs for immediate family, the ceremony would take place under a pair of shade trees at sunset.

For the reception, Kim and Michael wanted something casual but memorable, a distinctly West Coast party that would incorporate the bride's zeal for country traditions.

Most women would have found this event's overall logistics daunting—orchestrating a hundred details from another coast. Kim was chiefly concerned with just one major problem: lighting. "Dark" was the operative word when it came time to discuss the lighting challenge in what had been until now strictly a daytime venue. Knowing it would be pitch black after the sun set, Kim and her floral designer, Kate Stanley, began a plan of attack. In addition to the forty camp lanterns that would sit on the tables, they scattered hundreds of Mexican luminarias—votive candles set inside paper bags—around the site. The beautiful glow would not only prevent guests from crashing into the trees but, according to Kim, would act as ground lights that "described the landscape." A final fillip: the string of Japanese paper lanterns strung between two trees to illuminate the dessert table.

One of the reasons Kim was so relaxed about the details was

that she had one firm conviction: "When you're planning a wedding from another coast, pick professionals you trust, then let them do their own thing." She trusted her florist, Kate Stanley, implicitly. The two had known each other for years, having worked together at an advertising agency.

Kim's main objectives were simple flowers and muted tones. "The site was so natural, it felt contrived to bring in color," she said. Bride and florist communicated by phone, fax, and Federal Express. When Kim discovered a pair of antique sap buckets in a friend's New Jersey shop, she shipped them to Kate, who used them to fashion the arrangements that decorated the wedding site's shade tree. Kate also worked with the old camp lanterns that Kim wanted to use as centerpieces along with olive branches and lemons. She found a number of small celadon pots, one of which she sent to the bride for approval, and began planning arrangements of flowering herbs, olive branches, and garden roses.

Kim and Michael wanted dinner to be an elaborate picnic showcasing the region's remarkable food and wine. Biting into "the best tuna sandwich we'd ever had," the bride and groom knew they'd found a caterer from heaven. Skeptical at first about

hiring an outfit called the Jimtown Store, the winery's usual food provider, Kim and Michael paid a visit to the old wooden storefront that functions as the caterer's headquarters and café. Warm, quirky, bubbly, and "clearly very creative," Jimtown's female half, Carrie Brown, seemed like the perfect person to cater a wedding where food would be pivotal. Carrie and her husband, John Werner, who had been a partner in one of New York City's most innovative catering firms, ended up supplying not only food but style as well. They provided charmingly weather-worn chairs, a big beach umbrella to shade the cocktail table, and even a chauffeur—Carrie's father, who volunteered to drive Kim to the ceremony in his antique Buick.

For the music, Kim and Michael began looking for an old-timey jazz band—"kind of French, kind of 1930s." A number of agents sent tapes, every one of which was totally wrong. Then Kim turned to her brother, who described a band that sounded as if it had the nostalgic small-town appeal they wanted. So when Kim and Michael took their second planning trip west, they made a point of tracking down the Port City Jazz Band at a music festival. They booked them almost on the spot.

Inspiration from the past also directed Kim's choice of invitations. Searching for an emblem from another time, she discovered a turn-of-the-century engraving of a frog throwing his head back and drinking champagne. "Ugly in his way but quite elegant," the image made Michael laugh, which the bride felt was reason enough to incorporate it into the invitations, rendered in olive-green ink on handmade ecru rag paper.

The last choice Kim had to make was her dress. At first she didn't know if she would wear a wedding gown at all. A suit or a cocktail dress seemed just as appropriate. Serendipity stepped in during a lunch-hour visit to a lower Manhattan store famous for its great prices and high-profile labels. The Dolce & Gabbana dress she tried on—in fact, the first and only bridal gown she actually sampled—had a traditionally cut bodice, a billowy skirt . . . and a huge train that was totally inappropriate for a casual wedding. The dress needed so many alterations, from deep-sixing the train to changing most of the trimmings, that she spent the better part of two months riding the subway to her tailor in Astoria, Queens. Although the tailoring cost almost as much as the dress itself, the resulting gown was still a bargain.

FROM LEFT TO FAR RIGHT: The bridal party speaks; jazz tunes under Japanese paper lanterns; Kim receives a heartfelt hug; the head table.

THE DAY

Kim and Michael had wanted to avoid harvest week, when the sound of the winery's presses would have drowned out not just the vows but the band as well. Their choice approached perfection. The day itself was magnificent, and as for the noise, although nature had hastened the growing season, the owner turned off the machines during the ceremony.

Holding a bouquet of pale peach roses, Kim, on the arm of her brother, walked down a makeshift aisle formed by their guests while the Dixieland band played "Pennies from Heaven." Bride, groom, and officiant stood under a pair of oak trees, where sap buckets and antique market baskets had been filled with roses and wildflowers.

In his opening remarks, the officiant described how well suited the bride and groom were for each other. Then, instead of demanding to know if anyone in the audience objected to the union, he asked why the couple should be married, a question that elicited testimonials to love, fidelity, and patience. Following the kiss and "Strike Up the Band," the party began in earnest.

The waiters circulated with zinfandel-and-champagne cocktails, and guests got their first taste of the culinary amazements ahead. Guests sat on tree stumps surrounding tables made of wine barrels; normally used for picnics, they were transformed for the wedding with white tablecloths and roses, olive branches, and flowering herbs.

Like the kind of small-town supper you might recall from an old Italian movie, the evening was a seamless succession of delicious food, free-flowing wine, and jazz. Although Kim and Michael avoided some of the traditions associated with weddings—not a single flower was tossed nor a garter relinquished—they did honor the custom of the first dance, asking for "Stardust Memories."

At the end of the meal, a dramatic parade of waiters, each bearing a lantern and one exquisite dessert, entered the picnic area and placed their offerings under the row of Japanese lanterns. The wedding cake itself was small and chocolate, ringed by baby sunflowers. Finally, to prepare their guests for the drive down the vineyard's long, dark, and winding road, the couple distributed bags of chocolate-covered espresso beans and Gummi Bears. It was a final touch of whimsy—and a tiny jolt for the ride back home.

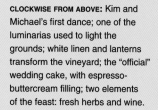

CLOCKWISE FROM ABOVE: Kim and Michael's first dance; one of the luminarias used to light the grounds; white linen and lanterns transform the vineyard; the "official" wedding cake, with espresso-buttercream filling; two elements of the feast: fresh herbs and wine.

on vineyard weddings:

› A GOOD CATERER WITH STRONG CONNECTIONS TO YOUR VENUE CAN SOLVE A HUNDRED PROBLEMS, LIKE ALERTING YOU TO POSSIBLE LIGHTING SNAFUS AND KNOWING JUST WHAT NEEDS TO BE BROUGHT IN (IN THIS CASE, ALMOST EVERYTHING). EVEN IF YOUR SITE DOESN'T INSIST THAT YOU WORK WITH THEIR USUAL CATERER, FIND OUT WHO IT IS AND INTERVIEW HIM OR HER FIRST.

› THE PARKING LOT OF A WORKING VINEYARD IS A BUSY PLACE, AND TRUCKS AND WORKERS WILL TAKE PRIORITY. YOUR GUESTS WILL PROBABLY NEED TO PARK IN A FIELD, SO TAKE RESPONSIBILITY FOR PROVIDING APPROPRIATE SIGNS.

› A BIG LANDSCAPE REQUIRES DEFINITION. MARK THE SITE WHERE YOU'LL STAND DURING THE CEREMONY, AND SUPPLY SOME KIND OF STRUCTURAL ELEMENT (CHAIRS, A CANOPY) TO INDICATE WHERE GUESTS SHOULD ASSEMBLE.

› IF SEATING IS LIMITED, USE "RESERVED" CARDS TO ALLOCATE PLACES FOR FAMILY MEMBERS AND OLDER GUESTS.

› RECOGNIZE THAT YOUR WEDDING MAY NOT BE THE SITE'S TOP PRIORITY—NATURE IS NOT GOING TO STOP THE RIPENING PROCESS JUST BECAUSE IT'S YOUR WEDDING DAY. IF THE ESTATE IS A WORKING WINERY, YOU WON'T WANT TO PLAN ON HOLDING ANY OF THE MAJOR ACTIVITIES NEAR OPERATIONAL AREAS.

› DRINK UP! IF YOU HAVE DECIDED TO MARRY AT A VINEYARD, INCORPORATE AT LEAST ONE OR TWO OF THE WINERY'S VINTAGES INTO YOUR MENU. YOU WILL FEEL CONNECTED TO THE LAND, AND THE VINTNER WILL APPRECIATE THE GESTURE.

› *PHOTO TIP:* SOME LOCATIONS BEG TO BE PHOTOGRAPHED IN COLOR, ESPECIALLY SITES LIKE VINEYARDS, WHICH INCORPORATE LOTS OF DUSKY PASTEL TONES AND SOFT LIGHT THAT CAN LOOK AS TIMELESS AS BLACK-AND-WHITE.

the professionals

caterer
CARRIE BROWN

NUMBER OF YEARS IN BUSINESS: Seven.

WHAT I LOVE ABOUT DOING WEDDINGS: Parties are fun to cater, but weddings have meaning for everyone involved. They're always joyous, always poignant. Helping to plan and execute someone's dream is a wonderful responsibility that I take seriously but with a spirit of fun and a desire to find a fresh approach to tradition for every couple.

HOW I WORK WITH A CLIENT: Some people find us serendipitously, driving around the Sonoma countryside. Others find us in magazine articles or have attended other events we have catered.

We usually meet at Jimtown at least once. We might taste an hors d'oeuvre or two, like olive salad with goat cheese, and have some iced ginseng tea. After the first meeting, we rely heavily on phone and fax to book rentals and staff, finalize the menu, and establish a schedule.

Once we define the concept of the food and service, we provide a menu, along with options for picking and choosing—more hors d'oeuvre choices than needed or a few combinations for grilling, with different fresh condiments. At this stage the menu will have balance and will be designed to make choosing easy. We might refine our menu a few times. This is the fun part—almost everyone likes to think about eating.

We always schedule one on-site meeting so we can visualize the flow of the event. It is a good idea to visit the site at the planned time of day of the wedding or reception. Physically walking and talking through the whole party, from hors d'oeuvres to cake-cutting, helps us determine logistics—like where bars and buffets should be placed—and prevents last-minute snags. If the event is outdoors, we want to make sure the head table is positioned so the couple won't be squinting into the setting sun and the buffet is set up in a place where the food won't cook again in the heat.

WORKING WITHIN A BUDGET: There are all sorts of ways to keep a budget in check. Sparkling wine or champagne isn't necessary throughout the event, but you'll want enough for an aperitif to be served with hors d'oeuvres. We allow our clients to purchase their own wine and spirits; wineshops will often give case discounts, and some might charge only for bottles opened.

You don't have to have four or five different hors d'oeuvres. Two or three will be fine as long as the cocktail hour doesn't extend beyond ninety minutes. Clients should ask how many pieces per person their budget can provide and they can ask for another inexpensive suggestion if the amount seems too meager.

Obviously, a plated sit-down meal with foie gras and lobster will be much more expensive than a brunch reception. Or if you're marrying outdoors, think about a fabulous picnic with the foods all prepared in advance. That will probably mean less staff, no grill chef on-site, and fewer formal rentals. Many rental companies, by the way, have several grades of china, stemware, and flatware. Whatever you do, don't sacrifice quality, and don't let your guests go hungry.

SIGNATURE STYLE: California countryside food—rustic, earthy, and lusty. Our menus reflect the season, inspired by the best-of-everything ingredients. Spring could mean baby rib lamb chops grilled in rosemary zinfandel marinade, along with pencil-thin asparagus that we might blanch for a second before adding it to a delicate melon-seed pasta. Our presentations are artistic but unfussy—not plated restaurant food. We use special antique pieces from the Jimtown collection to create buffet tables that are inviting still lifes, but never too precious.

A WORD ABOUT HORS D'OEUVRES: Hors d'oeuvres should be not too long in the hand and should be easily popped into the mouth. Guests are busy meeting and mingling, not to mention holding a drink while dressed in their best. Food at this time should stimulate appetites and conversation and not be too messy.

MY WEDDING PHILOSOPHY: Our goal is to make the food for every wedding memorable—the best possible version of each dish each time.

FIVE THINGS TO TELL YOUR CATERER

1. The date, number of guests, ballpark budget, location, and time.

2. The atmosphere, mood, and feel of the day.

3. Your favorite foods and how you hope to make the meal a reflection of your mutual style and taste as well as pleasing to your guests.

4. What your flowers will be like, so the caterer knows whether to use colorful garnishes or something simpler; the colors you prefer for serving dishes and props.

5. Special food requests for children and guests with dietary restrictions.

FIVE THINGS TO ASK YOUR CATERER

1. The cost of food, staff, and rentals. Is ice included? Are there hidden costs, like garbage removal? What portion will be taxed? Is tipping included or discretionary? If discretionary, what do they recommend and how do they prefer the tips be handled?

2. What is their policy regarding refunds and cancellations?

3. When do they need a final head count?

4. What is the level of service—how many staff will be present, who will pass hors d'oeuvres, how many bars and buffet tables are planned?

5. When do they need a deposit?

a castle on the hudson

KIMBERLEY MARTINS AND ALLAN DE YOUNG **DATE:** JUNE 8 **LOCATION:** TARRYTOWN, NEW YORK **CEREMONY AND RECEPTION:** THE CASTLE AT TARRYTOWN **MUSIC:** PACHELBEL, CANON IN D MAJOR; CLARKE, "TRUMPET VOLUNTARY" **READINGS:** SELECTIONS FROM THE OLD TESTAMENT **STYLE:** FORMAL **TIME:** 7:30 P.M. CEREMONY; 8:00 P.M. RECEPTION **NUMBER OF GUESTS:** 130

"Intimate" may not be the word that comes to mind at first sight of the Castle on the Hudson, a gray stone mansion built in the nineteenth century. But to Kimberley Martins and Allan de Young, established Manhattanites who'd been to dozens of big formal weddings, the forty-five-room castle seemed downright homey. Kim had called off an earlier engagement just two weeks before she and her former fiancé were scheduled to marry and had a fairly cynical view of the wedding process until she fell in love with Allan. He, on the other hand, is one of those stars-in-his-eyes grooms who wanted to be involved in nearly every aspect of the planning. Along with Kim's parents, the couple choreographed an evening that was formal but heartfelt, focused on both fantasy and family.

THE PLANNING

On the November night when Kim and Allan became engaged at an island inn, having a wedding by the water seemed like a wonderful idea. Reality struck the next evening while they were talking with Kim's parents, who had gladly volunteered to pay for the wedding—if it wasn't held on a beach. Kim's mother pointed out the problems of a seaside wedding in New York, where summertime means hours-long traffic jams in a complicated network of bridges and tunnels. Kim and Allan took a deep breath and considered whether or not they should forfeit control for the sake of the budget or pay for the whole thing themselves, ultimately deciding that sand and water could easily be replaced by a big lawn and shade trees.

As far as the timing, Allan and Kim were of two minds: he wanted to enjoy the engagement period, stretching it out until the next fall; she, having been through the process once before, wanted to "nail it and be married." And when the concerns and demands of two different families came to a head, the groom simply said, "Let's elope." After weeks of discussions with each other

Kim and Allan show what a few months of dance lessons—and practice sessions on subway platforms—can do.

and their families, having decided that July and August would be too hot and March and April too cool, the couple set their sights on a Saturday evening in June.

Once the decision had been made to eliminate the beach and to marry in June, every other possibility in the world seemed open—Kim's mother even suggested that they take fifteen guests and fly to Paris for the wedding. But the bride and groom had a pretty good idea of the type of wedding that would be right for them—medium-size, heavy on family and friends rather than their parents' business associates, in a place with warmth and personality. Looking for a suitable site within driving distance of the bride's family in Westchester County, New York, Kim and Allan began scouting locations, from the Brooklyn Botanic Garden to Broadway theaters. When the bride's mother mentioned an old manor she remembered in Tarrytown, the couple paid a visit and fell in love with two things: the storybook details like hand-hewn beams, vaulted ceilings, and stained-glass windows, and the director of banquet services, Paul Richards, who made them feel as if the castle would be their home. Although the building was undergoing massive renovations in its transformation to a small hotel

and party facility, Paul was such a professional, that they knew they had found the right spot.

After they booked their castle, the other decisions were easy to make. Kim had originally resisted the idea of turning into a stereotypical bride, but she found herself being seduced by much of the traditional wedding symbolism, including a religious ceremony (both bride and groom are Jewish), a tulle-and-satin dress that would suit a princess, and even dance lessons. The wedding party itself would be composed of family members and friends: the sisters of both the bride and the groom, Kim's best friend, Allan's brother, the friend who'd introduced them, and a friend from Allan's childhood. Since the women of the wedding party came in three very different shapes, Kim simply asked them to wear long black dresses—whatever looked best on them. The groomsmen wore classic tuxedos. Everyone agreed on cocktails and a seated dinner, which Kim was delighted to have her mother supervise, after making sure she ordered a plate of baby lamb chops for Allan to munch on before going down the aisle.

All of the remaining arrangements involved equal measures of vision and compromise on the part of the bride and groom. Since

the couple met only seven months before deciding to get married, the two families not only had to get to know each other, but they also had to get to know a future daughter- and son-in-law. Kim and Allan tried to keep lines of communication open—Allan speaking with Kim's mother about the parts of the day that were important to him, Kim talking with her father about limiting the number of his business guests, both bride and groom dealing with Allan's deeply religious family and Kim's less formal religious background. "Talking openly, especially with each other, is what kept us all sane and together," recalls Kim. They both agree that it is vital to "give your parents a chance to react." Perhaps the most impressive aspect of this wedding was uniting two families who had such strong feelings about their lifestyles and their children. "There is a fantasy that everyone is going to fall in love and become one big happy family," says Kim. "That is clearly something out of the movies, not life." The happy outcome was testimony to a couple who were strong enough to voice their opinions while respecting the importance of family and heritage.

When it came to choosing the flowers, Kim followed her mother's advice about hiring a florist, then laid down a single guideline—nothing "huge." For her own bouquet, she envisioned something small and delicate, the stems wrapped in satin ribbon. Allan, as expected, wanted to choose his own boutonniere—something different from the groomsmen's. Kim's personal style would impose itself most on the centerpieces: her apartment is full of candles, and she wanted unlimited quantities. While the florist originally talked about centerpieces of small votive candles, Kim envisioned a far more dramatic scene and requested table arrangements of tall, fat candles, a glowing sea that would melt and collapse as the party went on into the night.

With the food, the couple found that they had walked into a perfect situation when they found their castle. This was the first wedding the facility had booked—a red flag for most couples—but Paul Richards was patient and reassuring. In addition to laying out the evening's order of events, he explained that the kitchen wouldn't actually be finished until just before the wedding and arranged a tasting dinner at the home of the castle's owner, prepared by the chef who would be catering the wedding. With the bride's mother supervising the menu, Kim and Allan had no qualms about signing the contract.

To reflect her personality, Kim wanted a hand-painted invitation on a simple note card, but her mother, thinking of the formal evening occasion they had planned, voted for the kind of engraved invitations that smack of tradition. Again, a compromise was reached: engraved notecards were sent to the guests, and the thank-you notes featured charming watercolors.

So far the couple had adopted a fairly traditional course, but they were adamant about having music that "didn't feel like it was the wedding of the week." Visits to two bands—both referrals from friends—resulted in a meeting of minds with one bandleader, along with some very specific "don'ts": no line dances, no kitsch, no ringleader, nothing too loud, and one very special number—their first dance, which Kim and Allan rehearsed for months on subway platforms, since their apartment was too small.

A self-described "non-dress person," Kim had no idea what she wanted to wear. Going from one bridal salon to another, she even got her father to accompany her on one shopping expedition. "He was a good sport," she said, "but not very positive." Finally, she glimpsed "an idea of a dress" in a shop window and realized it was reminiscent of a Horst photograph that she had always loved. She took the picture to a dressmaker and then visited every fabric shop in Manhattan searching for the perfect pearl-gray satin for the bodice. The fittings—six in all—resulted in a boned and corseted bodice that, despite its completely unnatural construction, felt comfortable enough to dance in all night. Together with ten layers of tulle, the confection would have been as much at home on a ballet dancer as on a bride.

Allan may be the world's only groom who helped accessorize his bride's dress while being completely unaware of what it looked like. He went shopping with Kim for her shoes and even purchased an exquisite pearl choker Kim had remarked upon. Her dressmaker, Rosi, fabricated a tulle veil with small rosettes to complement the gown and also gave Kim a pair of antique lace gloves she had found in a flea market. "After all the bugging I had given her about getting the corset right, the fact that she was so thoughtful was incredibly touching."

FROM FAR LEFT TO RIGHT: Allan signs the katubah, the Jewish wedding contract; the huppah, decorated with tulle and ferns; a black-tie crowd surrounds the bride.

THE DAY

Having decided to spend the final night of their single lives apart, Allan allocated part of his wedding day to a massage, while Kim went for the "pampering thing." The bride and groom posed for photographs separately with their families before the ceremony; Allan ate his lamb chops, and Kim wiped off most of the gunk her makeup artist had applied ("I kept the false eyelashes but lost most of the lipstick") and deconstructed her hair. As she peeked over a balcony to where the wedding party had assembled, she realized with a sense of relief that she felt "very much myself."

On Saturdays, Jewish weddings must take place after sundown, so the ceremony didn't begin until 8:00. Following Jewish tradition, both of the groom's parents accompanied him down the aisle. Any fidgeting that guests noticed was more a product of clothing than of nerves—because he had lost weight, the tuxedo he'd worn for years was suddenly too big, and Allan found himself being married while pulling up his pants. His accessories, however, had been chosen with care: new silver studs, a brocade vest, and Bugs Bunny boxer shorts that Kim insisted upon.

Following the groom were the bridesmaids, in long black dresses, with bouquets of pale hyacinths. Finally, the notes of Jeremiah Clarke's "Trumpet Voluntary" sounded, and Kim appeared with a parent on each arm—her mother in silk pants, shirt, and shawl ("my mother was so happy to be wearing something with pockets!"), her father in black tie. Allan says Kim looked "simply amazing and radiant" in the fitted satin bodice and clouds of tulle; she carried a charming bouquet of lilies of the valley. As she approached the tulle- and fern-trimmed huppah (the Jewish wedding canopy), Allan walked a few steps down the aisle and took her hand. All the guests were paying close attention, but

as the groom explains, "Symbolically, I wanted us to approach the ceremony together, just the two of us."

Stone buildings usually stay cool, even in summer, but on this hot June evening, the thermometer would have challenged even the most serious air-conditioning. Despite the heat, all the players performed flawlessly. Allan's cousin, an actor with a good voice, acted as cantor; his childhood rabbi performed the brief service. Afterward Allan signed the ketubah, the formal Jewish marriage contract, and the party filed into the reception space.

Immediately after the ceremony, guests convened for cocktails while the wedding party and families had more pictures taken.

The waiters passed sushi and chicken satay; a platter of hors d'oeuvres was set aside for Kim and Allan, who were able to grab a few minutes to enjoy the food and some quiet time together.

While the guests sampled the hors d'oeuvres, Paul and his troops checked last-minute details in the dining room upstairs, where the kitchen staff was plating the appetizers and lighting the huge candles.

When dinner was announced, everyone headed upstairs. There was no receiving line, no amplified announcements of bridesmaids and groomsmen; instead, after the first course, Kim and Allan took to the dance floor as the band struck up "You Do Something to Me," and 130 guests witnessed a fully choreographed pas de deux, as the couple dipped and twirled around the room. After their dance, toasts were offered, the dancing continued, and the candles burned into melting forests of wax. Most guests left at about 1:00 A.M., but a few—including the bride's parents—gathered upstairs in the bridal suite to replay the evening, until the couple gently "kicked them out" two hours later. As Kim said to the group, "It's time to begin being married."

FROM FAR LEFT TO RIGHT: Latticework icing and fresh flowers decorate the cake; Kim, Allan, and a small mountain of candles; arm-in-arm on the dance floor; heading toward the bridal suite.

TIPS

on castle weddings:

› IF YOU CHOOSE A CASTLE SETTING, DRESS THE PART. YOU DON'T NEED A TWENTY-FOOT TRAIN, BUT YOU SHOULD MAKE THE MOST OF THE CASTLE'S FANTASY ASPECT.

› GO FOR DRAMA. SMALL CENTERPIECES CAN'T HOLD THEIR OWN IN A SPACE THIS GRAND. IF SKY-HIGH FLOWER ARRANGEMENTS ARE BEYOND YOUR BUDGET, THINK ABOUT A FOREST OF CANDLES.

› KEEP THE CEREMONY PERSONAL. YOU WILL DEFINITELY FEEL LIKE ROYALTY, BUT YOU ARE STILL TWO REAL PEOPLE WITH REAL FAMILIES AND REAL FRIENDS. EVEN THE MOST REGAL SETTING WILL BE RENDERED INTIMATE IF YOU ASK THE PEOPLE WHO ARE CLOSEST TO YOU TO BE PART OF THE CEREMONY.

› UNLESS YOU WANT TO BE REMEMBERED AS A THEME BRIDE, NIX THE KNIGHTS. THIS IS A WEDDING, NOT AN AMUSEMENT PARK.

› *PHOTO TIP:* DRAMATIC INDOOR SPACES LOOK MOST ROMANTIC WHEN THEY ARE PHOTOGRAPHED IN BLACK AND WHITE, ALTHOUGH YOU WILL PROBABLY WANT DETAILS, LIKE THE FLOWERS AND THE CAKE, PHOTOGRAPHED IN COLOR.

KARINA YORK AND DAVID BRODSKY DATE: AUGUST 16 LOCATION: PORTLAND, OREGON

CEREMONY: SAINT MARY'S CATHEDRAL MUSIC: HANDEL, AIR AND ALLEGRO MAESTOSO FROM

WATER MUSIC; VIVALDI, "SPRING" FROM *THE FOUR SEASONS;* MOZART, "AVE MARIA" READINGS:

SELECTIONS FROM THE SONG OF SOLOMON RECEPTION: HOWELL PARK, SAUVIE ISLAND, NEAR

PORTLAND, OREGON STYLE: INFORMAL TIME: 3:00 P.M. CEREMONY; 4:30 P.M. RECEPTION

NUMBER OF GUESTS: 50

KARINA + DAVID

AUG 16

As children, both bride and groom had lived all over the world—Russia, Greece, Germany, France. Both ultimately found their way to Oregon, where they fell in love with the healthy, outdoorsy environment—and with each other. Karina York and David Brodsky had one of those relationships that begins with running and working out together, evolves into a trusting friendship, and eventually becomes something they realize they can't live without. When they decided to marry six years after their first meeting (he slipped the ring into her gym shorts after a game of racquetball), this couple decided that rather than drawing on their family backgrounds, they would create a wedding that reflected their own lifestyle.

THE PLANNING

It was a wedding outside of Paris that pushed Karina and David's emotional buttons. "We saw a wedding reception in an open field, everyone sitting in their best clothes, eating, drinking, and having a wonderful time," remembers the bride. "We wanted to re-create that very European feeling on our own turf." Their list of requirements included tables set outside without shade or canopies, delicious food, wine, champagne, and their most intimate friends.

Portland attracts sports-loving people who are drawn by the mountains, the microbrews, and the relaxed work environment. For those who are shopping for hiking boots, there are dozens of choices, but fewer options are available when it comes to planning a one-of-a-kind wedding. For about "one minute" before they decided to hold the wedding at Sauvie Island, Karina and David flirted with the idea of a hotel. But although the Renaissance-style room they looked at was exquisite,

Beneath the cloud of tulle, the surprise of high-heeled sandals.

they realized that it had nothing to do with their individual tastes. "We would have had to choose from the same menus as everyone else, sit at the same tables, basically have a very nice cookie-cutter wedding." After some thought about the kind of party that would really mean something to them, they focused on Howell Park on Sauvie Island, about fifteen minutes outside of the city limits. It has no parking lot and no food concessions but is rich with rustic charm: a historic house, pastures, fir groves, grazing cows, and a "pioneer orchard" full of apple, pear, and plum trees. It is a place that summed up all the things that had brought Karina and David to Oregon in the first place.

After they found their fantasy setting, the couple set about gilding the lily with a visit to an antique shop owned by Yves Edmond Le Meitour, from whom Karina had started collecting little objects years before. Yves offered them the use of any pieces they liked, and Karina chose a Louis XIV–style settee, a pair of chairs from Normandy, and a leopard-skin throw—after making sure

that Yves knew that in addition to a raw outdoor setting, his antiques would be subjected to the antics of several young children. "I was thinking about kids jumping up and down on the furniture, and really scared that something would happen to his things," remembers Karina, "but he just said accidents would be good luck."

Finding the flowers was a result of serendipity. Karina discovered a true visionary in Beth Ford, whose shop, Flora Nova, is as close to an art gallery as a florist shop can get. The bride says she could tell from just looking around that she had struck gold, and she was equally impressed by Beth's willingness to listen to her ideas and suggest options that fit her budget. She translated Karina's vague notion of "fruits and roses" into fantasy arrangements of grapes, apricots, nectarines, apples, and figs in wide-mouthed glass vases. Then she mounded the arrangements with hundreds of pale roses and interspersed them with fruits and thick candles.

Karina's tight bouquet featured Sahara roses in palest peach surrounded by a cream-colored cuff, tied with silk cord. Beth suggested lilies for the two bridesmaids and a miniature version of Karina's bouquet for David's niece, Sarah, the flower girl.

Once again searching for an artist among professionals, Karina found one with food. Ignoring the advice of everyone who had ever hired a caterer, Karina shook hands and didn't even ask for a contract. One reason for her cavalier attitude was a simple gut feeling. Another was the fact that Barbara Baker, who owns Cuisine Bebe Catering, did such impressive preliminary work. During their first meeting, Barbara asked Karina to tell her about the foods the couple liked best. The next day she faxed over an imaginative summer wedding menu "full of all the things we loved," including wine from a vineyard Karina had mentioned she and David were crazy about. Karina offers high praise: "She's an artist who really, really listens."

A fellow student in her statistics class told Karina about her cousin, Polly Schoonmaker, a local baker who specialized in unusual cakes. In addition to Polly's exuberant personality, Karina was impressed by her willingness to do something completely original: a three-tier jewel-box Italian ricotta mousse cake reminiscent of a goblet she'd seen in a San Francisco antique shop, iced in shades of cream and white and topped with roses. Even a last-minute request by Karina for miniature apricots was met with as much good humor as a frazzled pastry chef can muster.

If Karina has a tendency to want control over details, David leans the other way. That explains the reception music, provided by an unnamed reggae band with a lead singer called Luigi. David discovered them playing at a restaurant and liked the fact that they were about as unlikely a wedding band as you're likely to meet. Karina had some reservations about the fact that their set involved political commentary ("Not too romantic," she recalls), but she knew David would talk with them about the fact that they were playing a wedding, not a rally, and let the fates take over.

Having devoted the lion's share of her budget to food and flowers, Karina was practical when it came to the invitations. Contemplating her smallish guest list, essentially casual plans, and the high cost of engraved invitations, Karina ordered the best paper she could find, purchased an old-fashioned fountain pen, and set herself to writing each of the fifty invitations by hand. Far from being a professional calligrapher, she admits that the fibrous stock she chose was a true challenge to fancy curlicues and fine lines, but she also says the entire process made her feel she was "really getting married." She offers a warning to other brides considering handwritten invitations: "I definitely underestimated how long it would take. At the end of the process, my fingers were so cramped I didn't think I'd ever write anything again."

Karina had a specific dress in mind from the moment she and David set the date, the kind of romantic tulle-skirted gown she knew from Degas's paintings of dancers. After scouring local shops, she and her maid of honor, Theresa, decided to try their luck in Los Angeles, where David's best man agreed to sit in on the proceedings. "I would put on a dress, walk out of the dressing room, and wait for their reaction. When Paul said, 'You look like a ballerina,' I knew I'd found my dress." The bride does acknowledge that buying a dress so far from home wasn't the most practical idea in the world, given the fact that she had to fly back and forth for the fittings, and that the UPS strike threw a final wrench into her plans. Ultimately, Paul agreed to escort the dress to Portland, even booking it a seat on the plane.

FROM FAR LEFT TO RIGHT: Candles adorned with roses and fruit reflect Karina's romantic theme; the flower girl wears a head garland of rosebuds and silk cording; the apple trees provide a delicate backdrop.

THE DAY

After a week of ninety-degree days and thunderstorms, August 16 arrived like a present, clear and eighty degrees. Even then, Karina spent part of the morning on the phone with the caterer, worried that the grilled foods they had planned would be too heavy for the weather. After Barbara reassured her that people do eat cooked food in the summer, Karina opened the box containing her headpiece, which had been delivered along with her dress just the day before. In a moment of panic, she realized it was the wrong one—a pouffy cascade instead of the single-layer veil she had tried on. She enlisted a local tailor to deconstruct it, and then she and her mother headed for the hairdresser.

Meanwhile, David was having problems of his own as he and his groomsmen spent the morning at the church, moving heavy construction equipment that a building crew had left in the courtyard.

Finally—makeup done, veil altered, bridesmaids in their café-au-lait dresses, and flower girl looking angelic in satin-edged organza—the bride took a step almost as risky as marriage itself: she let her bridesmaid drive her to the church. "She's accident-prone," explains Karina.

Electing to have a brief Catholic ceremony instead of a nuptial mass (though Karina was raised Catholic, David's family is Protestant), the bride was originally worried that the huge cathedral would overwhelm the fifty-person wedding. Her groom was the voice of reason who decided to make it intimate by gathering everyone into the front pews. After the priest gave a sermon about the real components of a beautiful wedding ("not the church, but the people's love for each other"), he invited the couple to light the unity candle, which Karina realized she'd left in the trunk of her bridesmaid's car. As she stared, horrified, at the priest, he stepped aside to reveal a small candle, which was duly lit. The service concluded with Karina walking down the aisle on a pair of legs "I couldn't even feel."

FROM FAR LEFT TO RIGHT: The cake, inspired by an antique goblet; the groom and best man take five; the flower girl goes apple picking.

At the banquet, tables were dressed in summer white, topped with the bounty of the natural world—apples, tree branches, and huge glass vases filled with fruit. Barbara's husband was manning the grills while the nameless reggae band played under the apple trees.

Over the next few hours guests sat under apple trees, made champagne toasts, and applauded when the band played Bob Marley for Karina and David's first—and only—dance. It was a sunny blur of photos, kisses, magnificent food—"I wish I'd tasted some!" says the bride—and great wines. From time to time, geese and ducks from the adjacent nature preserve appeared, but the borrowed settee was subjected to minimal abuse, and Yves ended up bestowing it on the couple as a wedding gift. As the daylight faded, things loosened up even more. Karina wandered from guest to guest, pulling her veil out of tree branches. She, the best man, and David lit up cigars and posed on a fence, which immediately collapsed. She says that the reception's highlight was just being together and seeing David so pleased. "He was grinning and glowing, the very picture of happiness. The wedding was our baby, our production, not about just him or just me, not about family conflict. It was just about us as a couple."

TIPS

on orchard weddings:

› ORCHARDS ARE PRETTIEST WHEN THE FRUIT IS RIPE, SO CONSIDER THE GROWING SEASON.

› IF YOU WANT GUESTS TO DANCE, PROVIDE A DANCE FLOOR. TELL THE BAND WHETHER YOU'RE EXPECTING THEM TO PROVIDE BACKGROUND MUSIC OR A REAL DANCE BEAT.

› HIGH HEELS WILL SINK INTO THE GRASS. PLAN ACCORDINGLY AND WEAR A LOW OR MEDIUM HEEL, AND MAKE SURE YOUR GUESTS KNOW THEY WILL BE STANDING IN AN ORCHARD.

› IF YOU'RE USING A COMMERCIAL VENUE, FIND OUT IF THE FRUIT IS SPRAYED WITH CHEMICALS, AND CHOOSE YOUR DATE ACCORDING TO THE SPRAYING SCHEDULE.

› CHOOSE AN OPEN AREA SURROUNDED BY TREES RATHER THAN A SPACE IN THE MIDST OF AN APPLE GROVE; YOUR GUESTS' HEADS WON'T BE THREATENED BY FALLING FRUIT.

› *PHOTO TIP:* PHOTOGRAPHING IN AN ORCHARD WITH PATCHES OF STRONG SUNLIGHT AND DEEP SHADOWS IS A TECHNICAL CHALLENGE. TO WORK WITH THE SHIFTING LIGHT, YOUR PHOTOGRAPHER WILL PROBABLY HAVE YOU MOVE AROUND A LOT DURING GROUP PICTURES. HAVE PATIENCE!

resource guide

(1) into the garden: CLARE + DERRICK

menu

HORS D'OEUVRES:

Wild mushrooms baked in phyllo, crab cakes with lime aïoli, Santa Fe sushi

BUFFET DINNER:

Pacific Rim seafood platter featuring Oregon rock prawns, Umpqua Bay (Oregon) mussels, Pacific tuna, and clams; grilled rosemary chicken breasts and grilled summer vegetables; roasted pork loin with rosemary; eggplant, artichoke, and Fontina focaccia torte; domestic and imported cheeses; baskets of rustic breads; seasonal fruit salad with Oregon berries and yogurt dipping sauce; couscous with golden raisins and pine nuts; three-cheese ravioli salad; Asian rice salad with julienne carrots

DESSERT:

An assortment of Moonstruck chocolates; wedding cake decorated with candied fruits, white chocolate squiggles, and gold leaf

DRINKS:

Full bar, Botari champagne, 1989 Oregon Pinot Noir, Timberline lager

caterer

Food in Bloom
2701 NW Vaughn Street, Suite 421
Portland, OR 97210
Telephone: 503-223-6819
Fax: 503-223-0327

baker

Polly's Cakes
269 NW 23rd Place, Suite 6
Portland, OR 97210
Telephone: 503-230-1968
Fax: 503-230-2397
Contact: Polly Schoonmaker

dress

Vera Wang Bridal Salon
991 Madison Avenue
New York, NY 10021
Telephone: 800-839-8372 or 212-628-3400

florist

City Flowers
6141 SW Macadam
Portland, OR 97201
Telephone: 503-244-3886

band

Soul Vaccination
Portland, OR
Telephone: 503-771-3306

party rentals

West Coast Event Productions
1400 NW 15th
Portland, OR 97209
Telephone: 503-294-0412

(2) french twist: ERICA + DENIS

menu

HORS D'OEUVRES:

Assorted crudités

SEATED DINNER:

Melon with Parma ham, fillets of mullet with herbes de Provence, rack of lamb, ratatouille, regional salad with goat cheese, tapenade, and baguettes

DESSERT:

Fantasy fruit assembly, corne d'abondance

DRINKS:

Full bar, red and rosé wines produced by the family vineyard, Rippert du Prignon 1994 champagne

invitation artwork

Henri Louis et Les Autres
11 Rue de Tocqueville
Paris, France 75017
Telephone: 00331 46224929
Contact: Nicole Pibeaut

party design

Roberto Bergero
4 Rue Saint-Gilles
Paris, France 75001
Telephone: 00331 42720351
Fax: 00331 40043806

garden design

Alain David Idoux
La Charaude
Telephone: 00334 90047241
Fax: 00334 90046178

(3) the palm beach story: KRISTINA + ROBERT

menu

HORS D'OEUVRES:

Parmesan cheese puffs, mini crab cakes, shrimp wrapped in pea pods, shiitake mushroom and onion tartelettes, truffle mousse pâté on apple slices, mini potato crisps with caviar and crème fraîche, crispy vegetable dumplings

DINNER:

Mini field greens with endive, mâche, Roquefort, and walnuts; miniature lamb chops; baked salmon with lemon aïoli; potato and onion gratin; pencil-thin asparagus; tomato and olive pie

DESSERT:

Wedding cake, heart-shaped butter cookies

DRINKS:

Full bar, French 75 cocktails (champagne with lemon juice and brandy), Grigch Hills chardonnay, Mondavi pinot noir, Veuve Clicquot champagne, café au lait

caterer

Palm Beach Catering Service, Inc.
1426 Keller Drive
West Palm Beach, FL 33406
Telephone: 561-833-1411

baker

Sweet Tiers
8779 South East Federal Highway
Hobe Sound, FL 33455
Telephone: 561-546-8822

dress

Geoffrey Beene at the Plaza
The Sherry Netherland
783 Fifth Avenue
New York, NY 10022
Telephone: 212-935-0470 or 935-0491

makeup artist

Nancy Habel
Book through: Cusick's Talent
1009 Hoyt Street, Suite 100
Portland, OR 97209
Telephone: 503-274-8555

florist

Scott Snyder Interior Design
Telephone: 561-659-6255

band

Denny LeRouxr
Contact: Ted Schmidt 800-972-108

tent

Sperry Tents
11 Marconi Lane
Marion, MA 02738
Telephone: 888-825-7542 or 508-748-1792
Contact: Tim Sperry

---

(4) just family: PILAR + STEPHEN

menu

DINNER:

Sautéed portobello mushrooms, salad, lobster, and steak

DESSERT:

Wedding cake

baker

Gail Watson Custom Wedding Cakes
335 West 38th Street
New York, NY 10018
Telephone: 212-736-0705

dress

Vera Wang Bridal Salon
991 Madison Avenue
New York, NY 10021
Telephone: 800-839-8372 or 212-628-3400

---

(5) african rhythms: RHONDA + ELLIOT

menu

HORS D'OEUVRES:

Spicy Caribbean patties, coconut chicken bites, plantain tarts, codfish fritters, vegetable spring rolls with duck sauce

LUNCH:

Salad with mango papaya dressing, jerk chicken quarters, beef roti, fried plantain, peas and rice, curried carrots, sweet potato pudding, johnnycakes

DESSERT:

Wedding cake, Caribbean black cake

DRINKS:

1996 Louis Jadot Beaujolais-Villages, 1996 Torresella pinot grigio, Cook's American sparkling wine, sparkling apple cider

caterer

Boca Raton Resort & Club
501 East Camino Real
Boca Raton, FL 44341
Telephone: 800-327-0101 or 567-395-3000

dress

Nigerian Fabrics & Fashion
701 Fulton Street
Brooklyn, NY 11217
Telephone: 800-ADEWUM6 or 718-260-9416
Fax: 718-260-9431
Contact: Jonathan or Gboyega Adewumi

site

The Morikami Museum and Japanese Gardens
4000 Morikami Park Road
Delray Beach, FL 33446
Telephone: 561-495-0233
Fax: 561-499-2557

event planner

Brenda Turnbull
18027 Rhumba Way
Boca Raton, FL 33496
Telephone: 561-477-5000

disc jockey

David Stanley
P.O. Box 95
Princeton, NJ 08542
Telephone: 800-278-1558

centerpiece sculptures and favors

B Group
Telephone: 888-225-4065
Fax: 908-359-0752

⑥ a gathering of clans: CAROLINE + STUART

menu

DINNER:

Mesclun salad, grilled tuna, whipped potatoes, haricots verts

DESSERT:

Wedding cake, custom-made floral mints

caterer

Chef Tonner Catering
P.O. Box 1145
Block Island, RI 02807
Telephone and fax: 401-466-2801

cake

Cupcake Café
522 Ninth Avenue
New York, NY 10018
Telephone: 212-465-1530

florist

Ned Phillips, Jr.
P.O. Box 404
Water Street
Block Island, RI 02807
Telephone: 401-466-5161
Contact: Mary E. Anderson

band

Book through: Wesley Wirth
Boston, MA
Telephone: 617-864-0454

 7 an american fiesta: MARIA + JEFF

menu

BUFFET DINNER:

Mexican and pasta food stations

DESSERT:

Wedding cake

DRINKS:

*Margaritas, Coronita beer, wine and champagne,
espresso and cappuccino*

caterer

Bird of Paradise
24 West Carmel Valley Road
Carmel Valley, CA 93924
Telephone: 408-659-3417
Contact: Jon Kasky

baker

Cakework
Telephone: 415-821-1333
Contact: Cecile Gady

florist

Clare W. Webber Florals and Events by Design
Telephone: 510-261-8606
Contact: Clare Webber

band

Napata Mero and the Chocolate Kisses
Telephone: 510-531-9300
Contact: Napata Mero

mariachi band

Francisco Ponce
Telephone: 408-225-6161

consultant

Laurie Arons Special Events
P.O. Box 373
Sausalito, CA 94966
Telephone: 415-332-0600
Fax: 415-332-0601
Contact: Laurie Arons

8 a christmas carol: CLAIRE + JONATHAN

menu

HORS D'OEUVRES:

Peking duck, smoked salmon, pâté de foie gras, chicken satay

DINNER:

Lobster, scallops, and shrimp in a pastry shell; salad with Roquefort dressing and walnuts; rack of lamb with spinach soufflé and julienne vegetables

DESSERT:

Citron, peach, and cassis sorbet; chocolate cake; wedding cake

DRINKS:

Martini bar, Bollinger champagne, Cakebread Chardonnay, Pouilly Montrachet, Grand-Puy-Lacoste

baker

Gail Watson Custom Wedding Cakes
335 West 38th Street
New York, NY 10018
Telephone: 212-736-0705

site

The St. Regis Hotel
2 East 55th Street
New York, NY 10022
Telephone: 212-339-6776
Fax: 212-750-9658
Contact: Robert Whalen

dress

Ulla-Maija
24 West 40th Street
New York, NY 10018
Telephone: 212-768-0707

florist

Stone Kelly
328 Columbus Avenue
New York, NY 10023
Telephone: 212-875-0500

band

The Bob Hardwick Sound
136 East 57th Street
New York, NY 10022
Telephone: 212-838-7521

⑨ making a splash: HOLLY + LING

menu

HORS D'OEUVRES:

Crab cakes with plum dip; scallops wrapped in bacon; spring rolls; endive with vegetarian mousse

BUFFET DINNER:

Grilled swordfish steaks; grilled beef filet; grilled vegetables; roasted new potatoes with garlic and rosemary; pasta with olives, capers, and tomatoes; green salad

DESSERT:

Chocolate cake with white frosting, decorated with fresh roses; sugar-dusted Italian pastries; fresh berries and cream

DRINKS:

Open bar, red and white wines, champagne

site

Bridgehampton Tennis and Surf Club
Ocean Road
Bridgehampton, NY 11932
Telephone: 516-537-1180

dress

Lisa Hammerquist
Telephone: 518-434-9151

hairstylist

Hairpeace
410 West 14th Street
New York, NY 10014
Telephone: 212-645-8333
Contact: Salvador Calvano

florist

Euphorbia Floral Design
274 East 10th Street, #2B
New York, NY 10009
Telephone: 212-529-4462
Fax: 212-673-6218
Contact: Sebastian Li

band

The Stingers
Book through: Debbie Wilson
Telephone: 212-769-0100

⑩ high mountains: GILLIAN + PETER

menu

HORS D'OEUVRES:

*Individual pizzas, potato galettes with smoked trout,
lamb satay, caviar-stuffed beggar's purses, sushi, summer
rolls, shrimp sukiyaki*

DINNER:

*Baby greens with Bosc pears and goat cheese in
raspberry vinaigrette; Chilean sea bass in port wine
sauce with morels; Bigwood Bakery bread*

DESSERT:

Bride's and groom's cakes

DRINKS:

*Magnums of La Doucette Pouilly-Fumé and Château
d'Armailhac 1994 Bordeaux wine*

caterer

Spago, Las Vegas
The Forum Shops at Caesars Palace
3500 Las Vegas Boulevard South
Las Vegas, NV 89109
Telephone: 702-369-6300
Contact: Tom Kaplan

baker

Polly's Cakes
269 NW 23rd Place, Suite 6
Portland, OR 97210
Telephone: 503-230-1968
Fax: 503-230-2397
Contact: Polly Schoonmaker

dress

Les Habitudes
101 N. Robertson Boulevard
Los Angeles, CA 90048
Telephone: 310-273-2883

invitations

Mrs. John Strong Co.
699 Madison Avenue
New York, NY 10021
Telephone: 212-838-3775 or 838-3848

florist

Floral Art
642 Venice Boulevard
Venice, CA 90291
Telephone: 310-574-6700
Contact: Jennifer McGarigle

band

West Coast Music Services
Beverly Hills, CA
Telephone: 310-278-6848

(11) rustic romance: SARAH + ALEX

menu

HORS D'OEUVRES:
*Vegetable platters, chicken satay, cheese platters, seafood
platters*

DINNER:
*Grilled salmon and prime rib, salad, Jordan Pond
popovers*

DESSERT:
*Pineapple upside-down cake, chocolate-raspberry cake,
ice cream*

DRINKS:
*Full bar, blueberry and ginger wheat microbrew beers,
red and white wines*

site

Jordan Pond Tea House
Acadia Corporation
85 Main Street
Bar Harbor, ME 04609
Telephone: 207-276-3316

dress

Morgane Le Fay
151 Spring Street
New York, NY 10012
Telephone: 212-925-0144 or 925-1528

band

The Boneheads
Book through: Skyline Music
Telephone: 207-878-2330
Contact: Marc Lourie

(12) lobster bibs for 170: TAMMI + PAUL

menu

HORS D'OEUVRES:
Seafood bar: oysters, shrimp, clams

DINNER BUFFET:
*New England clam chowder; lobster boil: Maine lobster,
chicken, corn on the cob, baked potatoes*

DESSERT:

Strawberries and cream, chocolate cake with cream cheese icing

DRINKS:

Full bar, beer, red and white wines, champagne

site

Corinthian Yacht Club
P.O. Box 401
Marblehead, MA 01945
Telephone: 781-631-0005

band

Sandy Martin
Amador Productions
P.O. Box 2067
Salem, MA 01970
Telephone: 978-745-7839

dress

Priscilla of Boston
40 Cambridge Street
Charlestown, MA 02129
Telephone: 617-242-2677

 13   home on the ranch: CHRISSE + JOE

menu

HORS D'OEUVRES:

Fresh corn cakes with smoked salmon; baby red potatoes with Asiago soufflé; warm Brie with endives and grapes on garlic croutons

DINNER:

Food stations: swordfish with corn-and-tomato salsa, wild-rice cake, and salad; Sonoma lamb skewered on rosemary branches, risotto with artichoke hearts, and Capressi salad (tomatoes, mozzarella, and basil); marinated Rocky Range chicken breast with rosemary; orzo salad with pine nuts and olives; green salad with glazed pecans and orange slices

DRINKS:

Carmenet chardonnay; Mario Perelli-Minetti cabernet; Morgan sauvignon blanc, microbrew beers, Maison de Utz champagne

site

Beltane Ranch
P.O. Box 395
Glen Ellen, CA 95442
Telephone: 707-996-6501
Contact: Alexa Wood

dress

Alençon
318 Miller Avenue
Mill Valley, CA 94941
Telephone: 415-389-9408
Fax: 415-389-8632
Contact: Nancy Taylor

florist

Kate Stanley Design
409 Tehama Street
San Francisco, CA 94103
Telephone: 415-227-4547
Contact: Kate Stanley

caterer

Elaine Bell Catering
393 West Napa Street
Sonoma, CA 95476
Telephone: 707-996-5226

baker

Perfect Endings
912 Enterprise Way
Napa, CA 94558
Telephone: 707-259-0500

band

The Swamp Dogs
Book through: North Bay Entertainment
Telephone: 707-224-0241

consultant

Mary Ellen Murphy Weddings
114 Glass Mountain Lane
St. Helena, CA 94574
Telephone: 707-967-0880
Fax: 707-967-0770

(14) vineyard vows: KIMBERLY + MICHAEL

menu

HORS D'OEUVRES:

Creamy goat cheese–and–olive salad; smoked salmon; crostini; jicama spears and local melons with chili peppers and lime

BUFFET DINNER:

Grilled baby lamb chops, rosemary marinade, fig–and–black olive tapenade; grilled cumin prawns; platters of balsamic roasted vegetables; sliced heirloom tomatoes with bocconcini (fresh mozzarella tidbits) and basil

DESSERT:

Chocolate cake with espresso-buttercream filling, zabaglione trifle with raspberries and blackberries, lemon meringue tarts, sourdough bread pudding with butterscotch sauce, cookies

DRINKS:

Iced tea, wines

site

Fieldstone Winery and Vineyard
10075 Highway 128
Healdsburg, CA 95448
Telephone: 707-433-7266

invitations

Soho Letterpress
71 Greene Street
New York, NY 10012
Telephone: 212-334-4356

caterer

Jimtown Store
6706 State Highway 128
Healdsburg, CA 95448
Telephone: 707-433-1212
Fax: 707-433-4252
Contact: Carrie Brown

florist

Kate Stanley Design
409 Tehama Street
San Francisco, CA 94103
Telephone: 415-227-4547
Contact: Kate Stanley

band

Port City Jazz Band
126 Madrone Avenue
San Anselmo, CA 94960
Telephone: 415-453-6369
Contact: Everett Farey

(15) a castle on the hudson: KIMBERLY + ALLAN

menu

HORS D'OEUVRES:

*Peking duck with scallion pancakes; chicken satay;
croustades of wild mushrooms with pâté de foie gras;
assorted sushi; cold-seafood station with shrimp, mussels,
calamari, octopus, and clams*

DINNER:

*Smoked salmon with apple chutney and warm nut bread;
salad of Bibb lettuce with edible flowers and goat cheese;
duck breast and grilled salmon, rice pilaf, and asparagus*

DESSERT:

*Wedding cake: chocolate cake with mocha buttercream
and lattice basket-weave icing; chocolate Dobos pyramid*

DRINKS:

*Open bar, Black Opal chardonnay, Rutherford merlot,
Jean-Louis cuvée champagne*

site

The Castle at Tarrytown
400 Benedict Avenue
Tarrytown, NY 10591-4330
Telephone: 914-631-1980
Contact: Paul Richards

dress

Studio Rouge
New York, NY
Telephone: 800-989-6368 or 212-989-8363
Contact: Rosi Zingales

florist

The Flower Barn
911 Addison Street
Larchmont, NY 10538
Telephone: 914-834-4900

band

Manhattan Swing Orchestra
New York, NY
Telephone: 212-765-8850

16 fruits of the imagination: KARINA + DAVID

menu

HORS D'OEUVRES:

Smoked salmon crepe roulade; bouchées filled with roasted pepper–and–artichoke tapenade

BUFFET DINNER:

Brie on baguettes with figs, apricots, and berries; salad of baby field greens with crumbled chèvre and candied walnuts; rosemary-skewered prawns and sea scallops; orange-scented couscous with pistachios; summer vegetable platter with fennel, green and yellow beans, sugar snap peas, zucchini, peppers, and mushrooms; Italian country rolls

DESSERT:

Wedding cake

DRINKS:

Champagne, Oregon wines

caterer

Cuisine Bebe Catering
2110 North Ainsworth
Portland, OR 97217
Telephone: 503-285-5754
Contact: Barbara Baker

baker

Polly's Cakes
269 NW 23rd Place, Suite 6
Portland, OR 97210
Telephone: 503-230-1968
Fax: 503-230-2397
Contact: Polly Schoonmaker

dress

Vera Wang
Vera Wang at Barneys New York, Beverly Hills
9570 Wilshire Boulevard
Beverly Hills, CA 90212
Telephone: 310-276-4400

florist

Flora Nova
1231 NW Hoyt
Portland, OR 97209
Telephone: 503-228-1134
Fax: 503-228-5335
Contact: Beth Ford